BEAUJOLAIS

THE COMPLETE GUIDE

BEAUJOLAIS

THE COMPLETE GUIDE

GUY JACQUEMONT and PAUL MEREAUD

FOREWORD BY
PAUL BOCUSE

Webb&Bower

MICHAEL JOSEPH

The English text in this book was translated
from the French by Anthony Roberts.

First published in Great Britain 1986 by
Webb & Bower (Publishers) Limited
9 Colleton Crescent, Exeter, Devon EX2 4BY

in association with Michael Joseph Limited
27 Wright's Lane, London W8 5TZ

British Library Cataloguing in Publication Data
Beaujolais: the complete guide.
 1. Wine and wine making—France
Beaujolais—History
641.2'22'094458   TP553

ISBN 0-86350-123-0

Typeset in Great Britain by August Filmsetting, Lancs.

Printed and bound in France

CONTENTS

INTRODUCTION

Nothing remains to be said, or written, about the Beaujolais. All the ground has been covered; in works ranging from slim academic volumes dealing with precise points to great tomes of composite history. For this reason, the literature of our region is exceedingly rich – in a sense, it is like a harvest of grapes, from which one may extract elements in small quantities, by the *tassée*, by the *pot*, or by the bottleful.

The Beaujolais has always had its lovers, poets, scholars, historians and painters. In our own time, the region abounds with famous men who do much to spread its fame and prestige; though a natural modesty on their part forbids us to mention their names. We are, however, at liberty to cite those who are no longer among the living, such as Jean Guillemet (with his Beaujolais Almanachs), Léon Foillard, Claude Geoffray and Jean Laborde. All these men are part of our history.

Why, then, have we compiled *Beaujolais, the Complete Guide*?

Perhaps because we feel that no

Guy JACQUEMONT

real letters patent for the wine of the Beaujolais yet exist.

More probably because the friendship between the two of us, born of a shared passion for the Beaujolais, has stimulated the wholehearted collaboration of many highly competent people in compiling this book.

For what makes *Beaujolais, the Complete Guide* special is the fact that it is not confined to the efforts of two co-authors. We have simply been the catalysts for a terrific chain reaction. Historians, writers, journalists, printers, wine-growers and wine-merchants have all contributed to this book, which is thus the work of a group of enthusiasts – not forgetting, of course, a remarkable photographer.

Beaujolais, the Complete Guide is like the wedding finery of a young bride. It is meant to glorify a *terroir* where men struggle and sweat to create wine which achieves the miraculous paradox of appearing both on bar counters and in the world's most famous restaurants. We have tried to make something of a firework display of this book and we hope that we have succeeded in shedding fresh light on our subject.

But who would imagine – especially in the month of November – that the Beaujolais has a past, that it possesses wines whose reputations are anything but *nouveau*?

People often talk about the Beaujolais' brilliant marketing methods, and cite with envy the unity of purpose shown by the entire region when each year's new wine goes out to be sold. Yet, during the nineteenth century, the Beaujolais won many awards, not only in France but at Turin, Brussels, London and New York, for its Morgons, its Chiroubles and its Fleuries. Many memorable dinners have been accompanied by these same wines, served on a basis of parity with the 'greats' of Bordeaux and Burgundy.

The fact is that the Beaujolais has been producing wines of prodigious quality for centuries, and the foremost names of French gastronomy have long been accustomed to serve them with their finest dishes. These are the *cru* wines that the growers and wine-merchants still seek to make better known.

Another aspect of Beaujolais creativity is shown in the labels on the region's wine bottles. We have made a collection of these labels, limiting ourselves to the creative areas within the region. Their diversity is astonishing: they range from the sober and informative to the portentous and parchment-like. Between these two extremes are a wide range of thematic labels, illustrating the countryside, the living environment, aspects of vineyard work, flora and fauna.

Throughout this book we have given pride of place to labels, and we would emphasize that we have done this not merely to display our collection, but as a way of illustrating the wines of the Beaujolais in their infinite variety.

Labels are full of life, after all. They represent the designer's art, the printer's craft and the grower's choice of decoration for his bottles. They acquire permanence of a sort because people collect them.

We have chosen labels which are still current, along with many that have passed into disuse. Maybe some growers now sell to different wine-merchants, or maybe certain clients have changed their suppliers . . . No matter, as long as the reader understands that time doesn't stand still in the Beaujolais, or anywhere else.

Paul MEREAUD

FOREWORD

Even when I was very small, I was used to hearing the word 'Beaujolais' used frequently, and I was lucky enough to identify what it meant at an early age. I must have been about six when I first went to the Beaujolais with my father to buy the celebrated barrels, *pièces*; my mother had 'put money aside' to pay for them. From September onwards, the main topic of conversation was the phenomenon of Beaujolais. Suddenly the weather assumed an overriding importance. My father kept a worried eye on the least cloud which might bring hail or storms to spoil the harvest.

It took me several years thereafter to sort out these early observations and impressions and understand the ways of Beaujolais, whom I assumed to be a very great man since we paid him visits, worried in case he got wet, and saved money for him!

So, one day in October we set off on our bikes to visit the Beaujolais, in a high state of excitement. After following the river Saône as far as Villefranche, we turned off towards Morgon through purple and copper-coloured vineyards dotted with houses built of golden stone. The first impression was favourable.

My father used to buy his wine at Morgon, from his friend Aufran, a former cellarman at the famous restaurant Léon de Lyon, whose creator, Léon Déan, at that time ran a wine business as well as an eating house. M Aufran and my father had worked together for eleven years, my father being the chef at Léon de Lyon. Daily consumption of Beaujolais in the restaurant ran at 220 litres or the entire contents of one barrel between the morning *casse-croûte*, lunch, dinner and individual glasses bought at the counter.

We arrived at our destination. After the usual polite greetings and enquiries after health and the weather, we got down to serious business. How was this year's Beaujolais coming along and – the crucial point – what was a barrel going to cost? Obviously, the price varied each year according to the harvest. The acquisition of these barrels represented a huge outlay for my father, because they had to be paid for on the nail. Some years, when business at the restaurant was poor, he found himself obliged to borrow from his brother (much against his will) to buy the wine.

Once this stage of the discussion had been completed, we went down into the sanctuary where Sieur Beaujolais was preparing himself for his arrival. A scent of wood, mingled with an odour of musty stone and humid earth floors, enveloped us; the atmosphere was cool and fragrant. Then the tasting began. One of the dried sausages hanging from the beam at the doorway was sacrificed for the occasion, along with some goat cheeses which were being dried and ripened in a wire meat-safe. The composite blend of smells delighted me and made me feel slightly giddy.

Finally, agreement was reached on the price and the day when the barrels would be collected. (A few years earlier, in my grandfather's time, barrels and tuns, *tonneaux*, would have been carried by a paddleboat named *Le Parisien*, which plied the Saône between Mâcon and Lyon, delivering its precious cargo as it went.) All these dealings led us to the bistro on the village square. This was a café-cum-tobacconist-cum-grocery-shop, where the official papers authorizing the transportation of the barrels were customarily filled in. Not infrequently, a local wine-grower would bring in a Beaujolais from the year of his birth, and the men would drink another toast, waxing lyrical about the 'gunflint' savour of Clos de Py Beaujolais (Clos de Py being the name of the place where the grapes were harvested).

Next came the storytelling: everyone vying to tell the best joke or real life story. Often these were the same year after year, but no one thought them any the worse and always laughed just as heartily.

The story that I remember best concerned the curate of Odenas, the village just beside Château de la Chaize. This memorable person, Georges Réthy by name, was later nominated to the parish of Collonges and presided at my first communion.

The curate of Odenas was no ordinary priest. During the 1914–18 war he had been a captain in a regiment of Chasseurs Alpins and he continued to wear vestiges of his military uniform while carrying out his duties as a pastor: puttees, beret and cape. He bore the insignia of the Legion of Honour in his buttonhole, and was as skilled in the use of the paint brush as he was at sprinkling holy water. Scenes of Beaujolais life were his favourite subjects for drawings and paintings. At the beginning of his time at Odenas, his relations with local men were uncertain, especially with those whose left-wing ideas were categorically 'red' (perhaps because of the wine?).

The curate's flock at that time consisted of women and children only. The worthy man of God would probably have adapted to this situation perfectly well, had it not been for an untoward incident.

One day, after some heavy rainstorms, the roof of the presbytery was found to be leaking. The curate decided to go to the mayor and village councillors for assistance. A

meeting was held at the town hall, beside the church, and the curate explained his problem. The mayor and councillors laughed and advised that he take a ladder, go up on the roof, and replace the broken tile – just as *they* did when leaks developed in their winery roofs. (It was, of course, out of the question that any water

should get into the Beaujolais.) The thing was perfectly simple and the curate could do it himself. The curate listened, thanked them warmly, and went home.

The following Sunday, as the women and children gathered on the square in front of the church prior to High Mass, they met the curate walking in procession with four choirboys in the vanguard. He carried his bucket of holy water and his sprinkler, and he was wearing his full Corpus Christi regalia. The little group crossed the village, watched by the entire population with a mixture of slyness and bafflement. Slyest of all were the men sitting on the café terrace by the church; the ones who never set foot in the House of God, who didn't hold with religion, and thought the Sunday services only good for diverting the women.

The little group made its way up to the spring which fed the village water tower. Here, the curate blessed the water, and all five made their way back the way they had come. When he reached the square, the curate addressed the assembled crowd of people. 'I am aware', he said, 'that you never put water in your Beaujolais, but as of this evening you will all drink soup that is made with holy water!' From that day onwards, curate Réthy was adopted as a friend by the whole village, no matter what their beliefs.

After these excesses, my father and I returned to Collonges. The following day, we began preparing the cellar for the arrival of the barrels.

For me, going down into the cellar was always a thrilling business, I

suppose because of the darkness and the shadows. The smells of must and sulphur would catch my throat, especially when the barrels were being fumigated. This operation was very exciting: my father would direct the tiny blue flame held in his fingers into each of the barrels, one by one. At last, the day of delivery arrived. Each barrel had to be roped and lowered down the stairway into the cellar. My father, standing at the bottom, had to stop the barrel's descent. This I thought dangerous in the extreme, and I was terrified that he would be crushed by the weight.

From this time on, the Beaujolais required much care. We had to check regularly on each barrel, as the wood progressively absorbed the liquid. At the same time we had to ullage the casks and draw the wine off the lees that formed.

Then came the bottling. So he could recognize the *cru* Beaujolais from the rest, my father put different coloured rubber bands around the neck of each bottle.

Plenty of Beaujolais has flowed across the world since those days. When I took over from my father, I no longer had to do all the work I have just described. My good friend Georges Duboeuf still does it all for me, under the best possible

Anne de Beaujeu:
benefactress of Villefranche.
(Detail from tryptych
by Maître de Moulins)

conditions; he possesses highly efficient machinery for every procedure, and as a result I receive the wine already bottled.

In the beginning, Beaujolais was a *petit vin*, known only to locals and to the people of Lyon. It was much favoured by men playing *boule*. I can still remember those sunny Sundays of my childhood, when my father would put the forty-six-centilitre jugs into buckets of cold water in the shade of the plane trees. Here the *boule* players would come to refresh themselves after a hard game, and be served by women in bright dresses.

The hour of glory for Beaujolais came on the day that a shrewd group of wine-growers brought it to Paris. It caught on immediately. Ever since then, the arrival of Beaujolais Nouveau has been celebrated like the birth of a baby; each year, the event grows in importance, as the reputation of the wine attains new pinnacles. Today it is known all over the world. I myself have contributed actively towards promoting Beaujolais in Japan and, more especially, in the United States. The agent who handles my distribution in the latter, an Englishman with a remarkable talent for public relations, had the excellent idea of organizing a carefully orchestrated annual twelve-day tour for me, throughout the principal states. At each stopover in a new city, a meal was prepared by us at the home of one of the foremost citizens. About a dozen people would be invited, including representatives of TV, press and radio. I would go out and do the shopping in person, accompanied by the lady of the house, and then we would do the cooking together. The meals were accompanied by Beaujolais (naturally) and the great *crus* of our region.

This formula produced more publicity than any five-hundred-seat gala could ever have done.

The following day, we travelled on to a different town; sometimes we went through as many as ten per tour. Like itinerant performers, each evening we mounted our show all over again.

In the same way, with my wine-merchants, I sounded out French-speaking African countries for several years, accompanied by our precious baggage of wines, *andouillettes*, sausages and local cheeses.

Everywhere we went, we laid on enormous elevenses, *Mâchons*, in the Lyonnais style, in the grounds of big hotels, serving the various foods and wines we had brought with us. Cool Beaujolais flowed by the gallon, to the evident delight of guests, hoteliers and nightclub-owners alike. The timing of the meals, at the end of the morning, was particularly appreciated, and the formula was highly successful in creating a new clientele.

Before us, Alexis Lichine, one of the main exporters of Beaujolais to the United States, had already made great progress by organizing trophies and competitions centred on Beaujolais wines. Closer to home, Jean-Baptiste Troisgros, serving Beaujolais cooled in ice-buckets, has made substantial contributions; and now every chef in the region is set on producing dishes that marry Beaujolais with local specialities like *coq au vin de Juliénas*, *oeufs pochés beaujolaise aux crôutons à l'ail*, *boeuf au Moulin-à-Vent*, *andouillettes au Beaujolais* and others.

Before herbicides began to be used on the vines, wild peaches, *pêches de vigne*, and blackcurrants, *cassis*, were abundant. A favourite wine-grower's

dessert was wild peaches sliced into a large glass, topped with a few blackcurrants and soaked in Beaujolais – delicious.

I am an unconditional lover of the Beaujolais, and I am now the lucky owner of a small vineyard in the region, at Létra. The wine-grower who looks after the harvest there, M Antonin Coquard, is president of the local cooperative winery; he has helped me to fill the gaps in my knowledge, by including me in every stage of the making of wine. This has made me feel closer to both vines and wine-growers, and I often go to Létra – whenever I can, in fact – to share the morning *casse-croûte* and exchange wisdom; for, in their way, these men of the land are great philosophers.

I remember a remark made by Joannes Papillon, during a trip to the United States organized by Georges Duboeuf and myself. We had invited along a group of wine-growers, and M Papillon was the doyen of the team. We were at the top of a New York skyscraper, on the ninety-ninth floor. It was about ten o'clock at night and we could see the city lights twinkling all around us. Suddenly Joannes Papillon burst out: 'But, the skies have fallen!' It was a perfect description, just as you would expect from one of those marvellous people, the wine-growers of the Beaujolais.

Today, I am deeply flattered to have been asked to preface this excellent book, which deals with the Beaujolais far better than I could ever do.

It was a shared passion for collecting wine-labels that originally brought together the two sponsors and organizers of *Beaujolais, the Complete Guide*, Doctor Paul Mereaud and Guy Jacquemont. The superb labels that adorn these pages are the fruit of many years' patient work, and they are admirably complemented by marvellous photographs taken by Pierre Cottin.

I offer my best wishes, along with my fullest admiration, to everyone who has collaborated on this book. The result is of a very high quality.
Et Vive le Beaujolais!

Paul Bocuse

The cloister of Salles

15

Jean-Jaques PIGNARD

There was once a shrub that could make men burst into song. Or rather, its fruit, when turned into a subtle beverage, had the power to warm their hearts and souls. It is said that the Lord gave grapes to Noah after the Flood, as a gesture of apology for having rained down so much water; and thus the vine and the juice thereof came into the world.

But when were vines first planted in the Beaujolais? Scholars still thirst to know. There is every reason to believe that the vine was established here as early as the Gallo-Roman era, before the Beaujolais existed as an independent entity. Mathieu Méras, a distinguished and erudite curator of the region's archives, states that the first document which explicitly mentions a vineyard in the Beaujolais dates from the year 956. The vineyard in question is that of Brulliacus, otherwise known as Brouilly; the mystical hill which, according to other less reliable sources, was shaped by the hand of Gargantua himself to guard the approaches to the vineyard.

Thus, when the lords of Beaujeu were campaigning beyond the Saône, they already had their Beaujolais to give them heart. In the same way, the bellringer at Rouen fortified himself with Beaujolais when he had to toll *la Rigaude*, the great bronze bell given to the cathedral by the Chanoine de la Rigaudière of Saint-Julien. The chiming of the bell was noticeably more joyous when the ringer had drunk *à tire la Rigaude*, as the phrase went.

The Benedictine monks of Cluny, who came to build a priory in the Salles valley, were also familiar with the cultivation of the vine. They liked it so much that they carved a bunch of grapes among the Romanesque stone capitals that still adorn their lovely cloister.

As to the treasure of the Templars, which is said to be buried in the Beaujolais district beneath the enigmatic towers of the Château d'Arginy, was it not simply the precious liquid brought forth by the autumn of each year, like Isis perpetually reborn in her cloak of pearly light?

THE BEAUJOLAIS UNDER THE BOURBONS

For over a hundred years, the king's close relatives held sway over the hills and valleys of the region without, for all that, attaching much importance to them. One of these Bourbons, Pierre, married Louis XI's daughter, Anne, maliciously described by her father as being 'of all the women in France, the least foolish', it being understood that there was nothing wise about her either. Anne de Beaujeu, as she is known to history, was regent of France during the minority of her brother Charles.

Anne bestowed the greater part of her patronage on the town of Villefranche, where she paid for the building of a clocktower for the collegiate church. In 1514, she designated Villefranche the new capital of the Beaujolais. Ten years later, her son-in-law the Constable de Bourbon betrayed François I and the Beaujolais district was annexed to the Crown, thereby losing its last vestiges of independence. Nobody much cared, for by now the hemp and grain trades had begun to enrich the local merchant families and bourgeois cloth manufacturers; the wine of the region, which travelled badly, was not yet a strong economic factor. At Villefranche, elegant Italianaté houses with turrets and balconies rose on either side of the main street. Indeed it was Italian architecture, as imported by the French kings following their various campaigns on

Habit de
Négociant beaujolais,

A Paris, Chez Nde L'Armessin, Rüe St Jacq, à la Pome d'or. Avec Priuil. du Roy.

Le Beaujolais
Touristique.
(*Map drawn by
H. Grisot*)

LE BEAUJOLAIS

MON BEAUJOLAIS

O Beaujolais, val ou colline,
J'aime à pétrir de mes deux mains
Ta rouge terre dont l'échine
Craque au soleil et boit du vin.

Chaque pays a son mystère.
Le mien rit, en biberonnant.
Le chais où mûrit la lumière
Ouvre sa porte à tout venant.

Mieux qu'un Palais ou qu'un Empire
J'adore un toit sur mon coteau;
Mes ancêtres l'ont vu reluire
Et mon fils apprend ce qu'il vaut.

Au pays des moulins d'en face,
La belle appelle son meunier;
Chez nous le grain pousse à l'audace..
Et l'amour veille en nos cuviers.

Fût-il seigneur en sa Bourgogne,
Nul n'est jaloux de son voisin.
A chacun selon sa besogne,
Heureux qui peut mouiller son pain !

Nous le mouillons tous à la ronde,
Tant et si bien que nos tonneaux,
Plutôt que de courir le monde
Se débondent sur nos tréteaux.

S'il me fallait partir en guerre,
Dans la musette du « mâchon »,
De ce Morgon qu'a fait mon père,
J'emporterais un bon canon.

Moulin-à-Vent, Chénas, Fleurie...
Et du Chiroubles... et du Brouilly.
J'en voudrais aussi, ma patrie,
Pour mieux t'épouser, loin d'ici.

Mourir ici ou là, qu'importe
A la raison d'un buveur d'eau !
. . . .
Il nous faut le sillon qui porte
La promesse d'un vin nouveau.

P. THOMANN
EXTRAIT DE L'*ALMANACH DU BEAUJOLAIS,* 1952

date to it. A charter at Saint-Vincent de Mâcon would seem to show that a hospice run by nuns once stood here, till it was pillaged in the eighth century by a band of Arabs, who raped and murdered the inmates; but this is not certain. And which King Louis was it who built the church and its altar? Nobody knows. It is, however, reliably reported that Julius Caesar pursued the fleeing Helvetic tribes across this pass, after he had defeated them for the first time on the banks of the Saône. They fell back to Bibracta, the Gaulish citadel at Mont Beuvray near Autun, where they were caught and annihilated.

GANELON'S BARREL

From here, drive back in the direction of Beaujeu. The road meanders, steeply at first, through the woods; then emerges to overlook the valley of the Ardières. If you come here at the end of May, or at the beginning of June, you will be astounded by the beauty of the yellow gorse which covers these hills. Beaujeu is at the bottom of the valley.

The entire landscape is dominated by the cone-like Tourvéon. Popular legend relates that Ganelon, the betrayer of Roland, had his castle on this site. A few remains may still be

The belltower at Jarnioux

GRAND VIN DU BEAUJOLAIS

CHÉNAS
APPELLATION CHÉNAS CONTROLÉE

CHATEAU DES JEAN LORON
DOMAINE DESVIGNES, LA CHAPELLE-DE-GUINCHAY (S.-&-L.) 71

12,5 % vol   70 cl

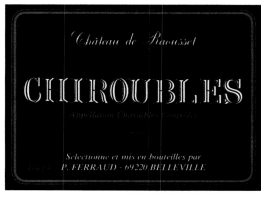

Château de Raousset

CHIROUBLES
Appellation Chiroubles Controlée

Sélectionné et mis en bouteilles par
P. FERRAUD - 69220 BELLEVILLE

DOMAINE DU PRIEURÉ
RENÉ PIN, PROPRIÉTAIRE

MOULIN-A-VENT
APPELLATION MOULIN-À-VENT CONTROLÉE

75 cl

MIS EN BOUTEILLE PAR R. SARRAU, SAINT-JEAN-D'ARDIÈRES, RHONE, FRANCE

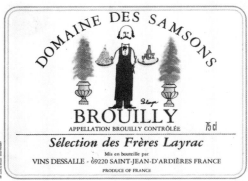

found on the mountaintop, but even as early as the mid-sixteenth century very little was left of any castle there might have been. The story is that Louis the Pious, son of Charlemagne, laid siege to Tourvéon to avenge the death of Roland. Ganelon, defeated and captured, was put in a barrel which had been hammered full of nails with their points projecting on the inside; the barrel was then rolled down the mountain. The Church of Chenelette is supposed to have been built at the point where it came to rest. Not far from here is Mont Saint-Rigaud, a place of pilgrimage which was formerly inhabited by a hermit rumoured to have special powers to remedy sterility in women.

But let us return to Beaujeu, whose centre is marked by an old half-timbered house opposite the Church of Saint-Nicolas. There is a legend attached to this place too. Apparently, up until the twelfth century, the valley was barred by a natural dam, upstream of which was a large lake. A son of the seigneur of Beaujeu, while hunting along its banks one day, slipped, fell into the water and drowned. The father wished to recover the body for Christian burial, but all attempts to find it were fruitless. Finally, the seigneur had the dam demolished and the lake drained; the corpse of the unfortunate youth was found at the

bottom, and here the father built a church which has survived to this day.

You are now in the valley of the Ardières, which is the backbone of the historic Beaujolais. The Beaujeu family never inhabited the town proper, preferring to watch over it from their eyrie in the Château du Pierre Aigue, which dominates the entire valley. On each side of the river as it descends from Beaujeu to Belleville are *châteaux* which formerly belonged to the seigneur's vassals, strategically sited to guard the road.

ALONG THE ARDIÈRES

From Beaujeu, take the road which meanders along the left bank of the river. This will take you past Lantignié, then the *châteaux* of La Tour Bourdon and La Pierre. The latter belonged at one time to M Garnier, to whom is attributed the discovery of garnierite, the nickel ore of New Caledonia in the Pacific. The road continues to the Château de La Terrière, a charming manor house which was of considerable importance in the Middle Ages. The next landmark is the chapel of Saint-Ennemond, once a druidic holy place. Up until fairly recently, anxious mothers used to come here to scratch the miraculous stone supposed to cure unweaned babies of diarrhoea. The

Vats at Château de la Chaize

Château de la Chaize. (Naïve painting from the time when the château was being built, between 1674 and 1676)

seigneurs of Pizay, a square-towered stronghold nearby, were traditionally in the (profitable) business of protecting pilgrims. A little further on, still on the left bank of the river, stands the Château de L'Ecluse which guards the approaches to Belleville. This fourteenth-century fortress belonged to the Garadeur family, trusty knights in the service of the lords of Beaujeu.

The right bank of the Ardières has just as many castles as the left. At the head of Vallée du Samson is the well-preserved Château de Varennes, a reminder of the troubled times of the late sixteenth century when Frenchmen were killing each other wholesale for religious reasons. At that time M de Nagu-Varennes led the Catholics in the Lyonnais region, whilst M Barjot, who owned the

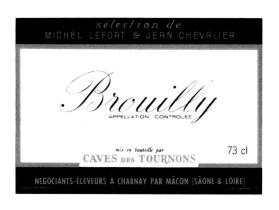

Château de La Palud, was a Protestant leader. The latter stronghold was only three or four kilometres distant from the former, which made for difficult local relations. Farther on from the Château de La Palud stands the Château de Saint-Lager, nestling in its village at the foot of the hill of Brouilly, yet which, along with its neighbour of Arginy, dominates the plain of the Saône. The Château d'Arginy is traditionally supposed to harbour the treasure of the Templars.

THE CELLARS OF LA CHAIZE

From Belleville, an excellent itinerary leads on to the Col de Poyebade. To reach this summit, the road ascends what might be called the sacred mountain of the Beaujolais, crowned with its chapel dedicated to Notre-Dame for her intercession against the plague of vine-mildew. The village of Odenas, through which the road passes, possesses more fermenting vats and a longer cellar than any other in the entire region. The cellar is no less than 105 metres long; while the vats belong to the Château de La Chaize. In the seventeenth century, the *château* was the property of the aristocratic Provençal family of La Chaize d'Aix. One of its members was Père La Chaize, Louis XIV's confessor, who gave his name to the famous cemetery in Paris. The *château* itself was designed and built by Mansard, while the French-style gardens were laid out by Lenôtre.

CLOCHEMERLE

Southward, along this road, is the small village of Saint-Etienne-La-Varenne, clustered on a peak around a charming little Romanesque church. Gallo-Roman tombs have been uncovered here and historians believe that Saint-Etienne was one of those fortified towns, well away from main lines of communication, used as sanctuaries by the inhabitants during the invasions of the third and fourth centuries. From here, the road continues along its winding way to Le Perréon and Vaux-en-Beaujolais.

Vaux prides itself on being the original of Gabriel Chevallier's *Clochemerle*, a novel eulogizing the earthiness, *joie de vivre* and good humour of country people. Vaux has also given its name to the river Vauxanne which begins here and winds peacefully down to join the Saône; but there is no wine grown here. Once you have crossed the 'Waters of the Vaux', a smaller road leads on to the village of Salles-en-Beaujolais, one of the area's great shrines, with its houses grouped around a magnificent Romanesque church and cloister. The latter were built by Cluniac monks, after the old Benedictine buildings and hospital on the island of Grelonges, on the Saône, were swept away by floods in 1300. The monks were later supplanted by nuns, on the orders of the Abbé de Cluny, and in the mid-eighteenth century the nuns were in turn replaced by canonesses when the convent became a chapter-house.

The aristocratic canonesses led a far more worldly life at Salles than their predecessors. Men were allowed to visit them – in all good faith – and many a love affair sprang up between them and the young daughters of noble families who came to finish their education under the canonesses'

Salles-en-Beaujolais: belltower and cloister

45

astride a ridge that stretches from Limas to Belmont. This ridge, which is chiefly composed of Jurassic chalk, is unique in that its oldest strata are on the surface and its most recent ones buried below. In other words, the terrain is upside down. The fracture that caused this geological freak is clearly visible as the Merloup valley; the result is a surface zone which is particularly rich in silex deposits. At Le Campinien, between Alix and Lachassagne, there used to be a number of stone-built factories producing assorted arms and tools.

THE OVENS AT ANSE

From Lachassagne, the road drops down towards the Saône valley, via Anse, which was once a Gallo-Roman *castrum*. The walls (third–fourth century) are still visible, surfaced with hand-cut stone. West of the *castrum* stands the fortress erected by Archbishop Renaud de Forez in the thirteenth century, with its two massive keeps. Anse, which originally belonged to the canons of Lyon, is famous for the oven that was once operated here on the principle that every customer brought his own dough to make his own bread. The man who tended the oven would take a handful of dough as payment, and the housewives would wait on the premises till their loaves were baked. The story goes that these ladies would pass the time by challenging any passing male to prove his virility on the spot; if he failed to do so, he received the same treatment as Abelard. There is even a rumour that an archbishop was put to this exacting test. To this day, the people of Anse refer to a woman of doubtful virtue as having passed '*devant le four*', ('in front of the oven').

Do not leave Anse without making a foray across the Saône to visit the old Château de Saint-Bernard, another stronghold which formerly belonged to the canons of Lyon, and the delightful little Gothic church opposite. Suzanne Valadon lived for years in this *château* with Utter and her son Utrillo. Today it is the property of M Lafoy.

THE BANKS OF THE SAÔNE

From Anse, take the RN6 northward past Villefranche. Beside the Saône, the Château de Boistrait stands guarding the Gué de Grelonges, a much frequented pass in Roman times. Further on is the large market town of Saint-Georges-de-Reneins, clustered around its Romanesque church. If you take the road to Montmerle, you will see the Marze family's small moated manor house. When you reach Belleville again, spare some time to visit the lovely collegiate church. This pure Romanesque building was completed in eleven years by Humbert III of Beaujeu. The seventeenth-century hospital nearby still has quarters set aside for old people, in imitation of the Hospices de Beaune. There is a single difference: the rooms at Belleville are still in use.

The road has now gone nearly full circle, back to the boundary stone mentioned at the start of this chapter. The final stretch leads past d'Ardières, with the Château de l'Ecluse nestled in woodlands close by. Turn left by the Voisin

46

monument for a visit to the well-preserved mediaeval Château de Corcelles; or, if you prefer, take the right fork to Drace, whose Romanesque church was ceded to the Abbey of Savigny around 1030. Here the tour ends. I have made no mention of monuments and beauty spots, but I hope that this brief outline will sharpen the visitor's curiosity and encourage him to make his own explorations.

THE VINES AND THE MEN

Georges GRUAT

The Beaujolais was in a desperate state. Domestic animals wandered aimlessly by the roadsides, driven out by their owners who no longer had food for them. Imagine, the wine-growers of the Beaujolais, a race renowned for their hospitality, beating their livestock from their doors like barbarians! These were the scenes described in the journal *Lyon Viticole* in 1880.

At that time, wine was vanishing from cafés and restaurants all over France; down in the *Rouge Midi*, people were up in arms against bootleggers peddling moonshine made from industrial alcohol. The Beaujolais had also tried to formulate some kind of collective protest, but in the end the wine-growers were forced to desert their vineless properties and make their way to the cities in search of work. Anything rather than die of despair beside vineyards being devoured before their eyes by billions of aphids, the dreaded phylloxera from America. Older men in the north of the region could still remember the 'endless winter' of fifty years before, when another plague had struck the Romanèche, Chénas and Saint-Amour areas. At that time, the temptation to burn the infested vines had been very strong; there seemed to be no other way of fighting the wretched pyralis. A storm struck the procession of boats across the Saône and quickly turned the pilgrimage to Notre-Dame du Ver

into a catastrophe; it looked as if even heaven had abandoned them. But then Benoît Raclet, in his little house at Romanèche-Thorins, stumbled on the simplest of remedies for pyralis: that of spraying the vines with boiling water during the winter. To begin with, Raclet was accused of witchcraft, but the evidence of his success soon proved irrefutable. The storehouses of the region, which for fifteen years had held only a few miserable quarter casks, once again were redolent with the good smell of Beaujolais wine.

After pyralis, phylloxera. It was written, said some, in Genesis, the

first book of the Bible: 'Thou shall plant thy vine and cultivate it, but no wine shall thou drink, for the worms shall consume it'. Why struggle against the will of the Lord? But Victor Pulliat, an ampelographer living at Chiroubles and son of a wine-grower, refused to listen to such nonsense. He decided to wage total war against the epidemic. Pulliat conducted a series of experiments, pooled his results with those of other researchers like Millardet, Vialla and Planchon, and one day discovered that phylloxera could be overcome by grafting on to American rootstock. This breakthrough gave new hope to the wine-growers, who wished only to live on their land according to the cycle of the seasons. The work might be hard and thankless, but they loved their vines like their own children.

The Beaujolais took twenty years to recover from the devastation of phylloxera. And then, quite suddenly, the region found itself crushed by overproduction. The 1900 harvest yielded 200 hectolitres per hectare, leading to a collapse in prices. The value of the harvested grapes was so low that it was uneconomical to pick them. The system had to be completely reorganized all over again, and at the same time a host of new diseases had to be faced: mildew, oidium, black rot, grey rot . . . Nothing was ever certain. Generation followed generation, each adding its own contribution to the structure of the Beaujolais. Thousands of wine-growers still carried out the same ancestral work, but now modern techniques made it possible for one dedicated man to work six hectares of vines on his own. (Prior to the First World War, the maximum had been two and a half hectares.) Furthermore, an organized professional structure was now in place to handle the marketing of Beaujolais as a highly appreciated wine. As Louis Orizet said, the region had 'deserved its victory'. But let us

JULIÉNAS
APPELLATION CONTRÔLÉE
DOMAINE DE LA VIEILLE ÉGLISE
12,5 % vol.   70 cl
PAUL LORON
PROPRIÉTAIRE A JULIÉNAS
Mis en bouteille par E. LORON et Fils - Pontanevaux (France)

FLEURIE
APPELLATION FLEURIE CONTRÔLÉE
75 cl   DOMAINE DE LA CÔTE D'ADULE
Mis en bouteille dans la région de production par
PASQUIER-DESVIGNES
NÉGOCIANT-ÉLEVEUR A SAINT-LAGER (RHÔNE) FRANCE

now turn to the vineyards and the men of today's Beaujolais.

PLANTING A BEAUJOLAIS VINEYARD

The black Gamay grape, with its clear white juice, was rejected in the seventeenth century by the aldermen of Mâcon. Its revenge was swift, for this vine was found to be equally at home both in the clay-lime of the southern Beaujolais and in the granitic soil of the north. But the Gamay is also extremely demanding. It needs ground that is free of threadworms and root remains. Before the appearance of agricultural chemicals, the only way this could be achieved was by resting the soil for five years. Since the wine-growers had to make some kind of living in the meantime, it was common practice to turn out dairy cattle on the fields for the five-year period. This practice also offered a margin of profit from milk sales when wine prices were depressed.

Thus, for many years, wine and milk were the staples of the Beaujolais region; and indeed it was a Beaujolais wine-grower, Benoît Aurion, who created the basic milk-marketing organization of all France. Today, economic changes have banished the dairy cow from the Beaujolais and the soil is now disinfected more rapidly by a fumigation process. But the land must first be sub-soiled, a back-breaking job facetiously known as mine clearance, *déminage*. This operation has changed considerably over the years.

At the beginning of the century, there was no alternative to the spade; but it took plenty of sweat to sub-soil one hectare to a depth of twenty-five centimetres. When animal draught methods appeared around 1912, the older inhabitants could scarcely believe their eyes. Beside themselves with rage, they fumed that horse, men and plough would all drop down dead – but, nonetheless, the method proved much less exhausting and the poorest wine-growers, who couldn't afford horses, harnessed their cows to the plough. Then came mechanization; winches were used for the steepest inclines, along with the famous double-furrow trenching ploughs, *charrues dauphinoises*.

In the classic process of preparation, when the sub-soiling is finished, the ground is rolled and the clods are broken up, as for an ordinary seedbed. It is much improved thereby and is ready to receive grafted rootstock which will have nothing to fear from phylloxera.

But the wine-grower's trials are not yet at an end. Now he has to set to with the dibber, *plantoir*, and dig 10,000 holes per hectare to plant his vines – more expenditure of effort. Meanwhile, in the laboratories, oenologists and technicians seek to perfect planting methods while lightening the wine-grower's labours – with such innovations as the grafted plant in its pot, to be placed directly in the soil surrounded with its own chunk of turf.

After planting, it takes four years before the first grapes are harvested in an *appellation d'origine controlée* (guaranteed vintage). But all through those years the vines must be taken care of: they have to be treated against mildew and oidium from the first year onward; then propped with stakes, *palissage*; then treated again to ward off fruitworm.

PRUNING POINTS

The benefits of chemistry cannot be praised enough, for the use of weedkillers has totally changed viticultural methods. No longer does the earth around vines have to be ridged up after the harvest is over and no longer does the piled soil have to be cleared away from the plants prior to pruning. The hoe has been virtually superannuated. The

panniers which were formerly used to bring earth up into the vineyards are now relegated to the status of old-fashioned accessories.

Yet the wine-grower himself is by no means inactive. The disappearance of his old chores has come hand in hand with a new need for him to cultivate as much land as possible in order to earn a decent living. And no machine will ever be invented to replace the human hand in the matter of pruning vines. . . .

A grafting workshop

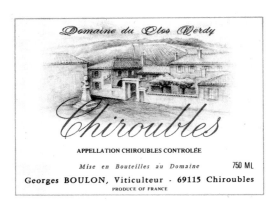

Domaine du Clos Verdy

Chiroubles

APPELLATION CHIROUBLES CONTRÔLÉE

Mise en Bouteilles au Domaine   750 ML

Georges BOULON, Viticulteur - 69115 Chiroubles

PRODUCE OF FRANCE

BOUTEILLE
№ 792269

La Cornaline

CHENAS

APPELLATION CHENAS CONTRÔLÉE

mis en bouteilles par

J.-C. OLLIVON   75 cl

NÉGOCIANT-ÉLEVEUR A ROMANÈCHE-THORINS (SAONE-ET-LOIRE)

CHATEAU DES GRANGES
BEAUJOLAIS

APPELLATION BEAUJOLAIS CONTRÔLÉE

Comte H. de RAMBUTEAU, Propriétaire

MIS EN BOUTEILLE PAR   **THORIN**   F 71570 PONTANEVAUX

Produce of France

37,5cl

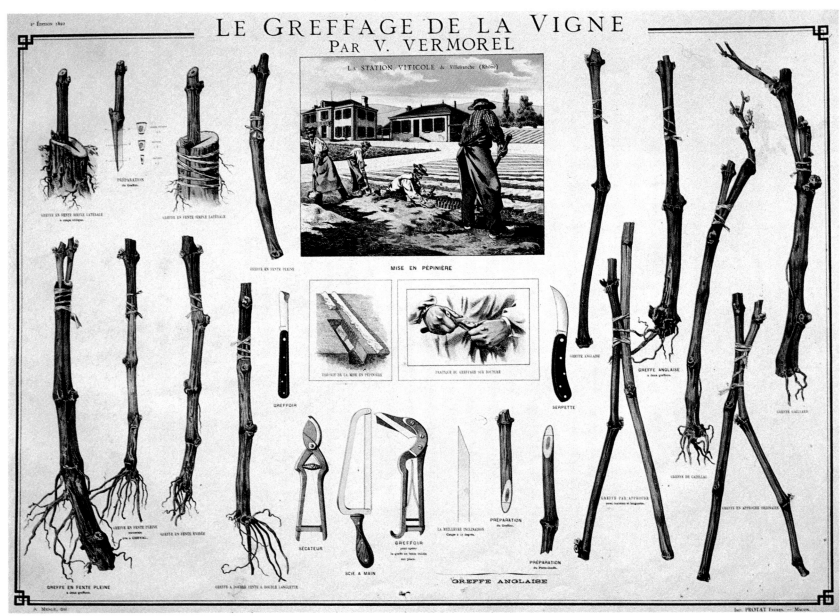

LE GREFFAGE DE LA VIGNE
PAR V. VERMOREL

VIN DE FRANCE

DOMAINE DE LA CHIZE

Beaujolais-Villages

APPELLATION BEAUJOLAIS-VILLAGES CONTRÔLÉE

MIS EN BOUTEILLE DANS LA RÉGION DE PRODUCTION PAR   75 cl

J. PELLERIN - SAINT-GEORGES-DE-RENEINS (RHÔNE) FRANCE

"CUVÉE DAILLY"

BEAUJOLAIS BLANC

APPELLATION BEAUJOLAIS BLANC CONTRÔLÉE

MIS EN BOUTEILLE A LA CHAPELLE-DE-GUINCHAY PAR LE

CLUB FRANÇAIS DU VIN   75 cl

LANCIÉ (RHÔNE) 69220

Beaujolais-Villages

APPELLATION CONTRÔLÉE   75cl

Réserve du Gouverneur Militaire de Lyon

ÉCLAIR N°1

ORANGE DOUBLE EFFET

TRIPLEX

BLOIS

JUPITER

NABO

During the long autumn and winter months, the wine-grower must work outside in his vineyard, despite the cold which numbs and swells his fingers in the morning mist. And pruning is no easy matter; it requires long experience and a deep knowledge of vines. The plant must be coaxed to produce its best; at the same time its twelve 'eyes', or pruning points, must be retained, since twelve 'eyes' are the maximum allowable for the vintage. But pruning must also be carried out with a view to what is planned for the following year. In many respects, the harvest depends on efficient pruning methods. For months on end, the wine-grower has to stay stooped in the most back-breaking of postures, tirelessly squeezing away at his secateurs. This is a terrible chore that no technician or academic will ever succeed in eliminating. It constitutes the tribute which must be paid to the land by men and women who live in partnership with nature. Recently, an inventive Quincié wine-grower named Jean-Charles Pivot (brother of the French TV personality Bernard Pivot) invented a chair which takes away some of the back pain from which all his colleagues suffer. But never presume to call the other M Pivot an 'armchair pruner'! . . .

SUMMER IN THE VINEYARD

When spring comes, *le printemps en fleur qui sur ses pantoufles brille*, as Verlaine puts it, the vine begins to sprout and sprawl vigorously. It must be soothed and to this purpose the sterile buds which produce over-abundant foliage are cut back. This process is called trimming, *émondage*.

At this stage, the vine is as fragile as a baby and requires enormous care. From the beginning of spring until the grapes are ripe, it is a constant prey to mildew. This disease, like the rootstock of modern vines, originally came from America. The spraying of a copper sulphate solution, *bouillie bordelaise*, has so far held mildew in check, and remains *de rigueur* in spite of other progress in the field. But other assorted fungi and insects still threaten, such as oidium,

SULFATAGES

Divisé par le jet, le sulfate cuisant
En pleuvant sur les ceps rejaillit et crépite :
Innombrables versets que la vigne récite,
En jetant son parfum en offrande au printemps.

Ainsi, sur le satin des feuilles ponctuées,
Que ne rongera plus le mal insidieux,
Se posent, au hasard, par légères nuées,
De frêles oiselets et des papillons bleus.

PIERRE AGUÉTANT
EXTRAIT DU *POÈME DU BEAUJOLAIS*, 1922

a real scourge to the wine-growers of former times who built the chapel of Notre-Dame de Brouilly to protect against it; black rot, which produces lesions; leaf-devouring red spiders; and, finally, grey rot, a fungus which attacks the grapes.

For more than six months of the year the wine-grower is engaged in a ceaseless struggle, scrupulously observing the advice of technicians for each treatment of his vines. And this chemical warfare is expensive, though its techniques have evolved over the years. The first back-pack sprayers were manufactured in the factories of a Villefranche industrialist named Victor Vermorel. Compressors appeared during the 1950s. These contraptions completely changed spraying methods and were a great boon to all viticulturists.

> Sans crainte de pressoir, le pampre tout l'été
> Boit les doux présents de l'Aurore.
> (All summer long, the vine branch drinks
> the dawn's soft dew, and never dreads the press.)

The vine flowers at the same time as the lily; a hundred days later, the start of the grape harvest will be proclaimed. This is an anxious moment for the wine-grower, who during this period is completely at the mercy of the elements.

Meanwhile the vine grows and grows, spreading out over the ground 'like a cat on heat' as the French

Scalding the vines (pastel from the Musée Raclet)

phrase goes. It must be lifted and tied up with withies, so that it can keep its queenly carriage and avoid being crushed by the wheels of the tractor moving along the rows. This is a long job which involves the whole family, boys and girls included.

The weather can never be counted on, given the constant threat of hail. Many a wine-grower has watched helplessly, with tears in his eyes, as the hailstones slash down, ripping foliage to shreds, bruising grapes and tearing the wood from the vines. What can be done? Nothing. Every possible solution has been attempted in the Beaujolais. The effect of

prayers having proven strictly relative, bells were rung when hail threatened. Then cannons and rockets were tried, to no avail: the hail still came down.

After a series of particularly violent storms, a defence association was formed, which decided to take extreme measures and use aeroplanes to spray the stormclouds with silver iodide. There was something to be said for this system, but it would have required the use of dozens of aircraft. As Papa Bréchard commented, 'Maybe we should go back to prayers. At least they wouldn't cost so much.'

Thus the Beaujolais abandoned the idea of aerial defence against hail, but not before some local wags had persuaded a young journalist, on the look-out for a story, that the most effective Beaujolais preventive was the systematic painting of each vineleaf with silver iodide. When the newspaper was shown to President Lavarenne, he nearly choked to death.

Finding themselves unable to defend their vines, the wine-growers of the Beaujolais decided at least to defend their revenues. They therefore invented a 'hail insurance' system, based on solidarity – the only one in France.

THE GRAPE HARVEST

Down on the *autoroute*, on the eastern edge of the Beaujolais, the holidaymakers are roasting in their

cars. The long ribbon of traffic undulates like the wave of conscripts from Villefranche, but no wine-grower would dream of joining it. For him, the holiday period is the time when he puts the finishing touches to his vines: the paring, *rognage*, which he does twice with his shears, to cut out over-abundant foliage.

Summer sinks into September, with its dust-clouds and morning mists. . . .

This is the most critical moment of the year. The right moment must be chosen to proclaim the beginning of the harvest, the right day selected for each patch of vines, according to the state of the grapes and the results of tests carried out by the technicians. In spite of many worries still to come, the harvest brings the wine-grower's reward. *Allez Pierette, va prendre ta serpette!* In the old days, when the vineyards were relatively small, most of the labour of harvesting fell to the wine-grower's families and immediate neighbours. A helping hand with the grapes, as with the corn at threshing time, was paid for by a good meal and reciprocated during the neighbour's harvest. The owners of large vineyards went down to the village square where harvesters could be hired every morning. Hard bargains were driven over the price of a day's work, but the men selling their services were grafters who thought nothing of starting at dawn to put in a twelve- or fourteen-hour day among the vines.

Between the wars, when the vineyards were beginning to develop and expand, the Beaujolais discovered the mining folk of Montceau-les-Mines. These people were mostly Polish by origin, deep drinkers but good workers; they spent their holidays (paid for by the Socialist Popular Front) harvesting grapes in the Beaujolais. In each 'cut', *'coupée'* (ie group of twelve workers harvesting one hectare in a day), blond, laughing girls from the Polish black country stood picking grapes and singing ditties from their faraway homeland. They would only straighten their backs to call out *jarlot!* for the vat carrier when their buckets were full.

In the 1960s the Beaujolais went through a period when harvesters were scarce. There were no job-seekers to be found jostling around the doors of town halls, as in the euphoric days of 'economic expansion'. . . .

Then came the students, mostly foreign, who were attracted by the promise of 'first-hand experience of the working world'. With their long hair and their guitars slung over their shoulders, they came down to the Beaujolais to sample the wine-grower's warm hospitality and the solid early-morning snack, *casse-croûte*. And yesterday's hippies have become today's friends. The wine-growers remain much attached to student labour, which is now all the more loyal since many owners have fixed up comfortable lodgings with

A hail cannon

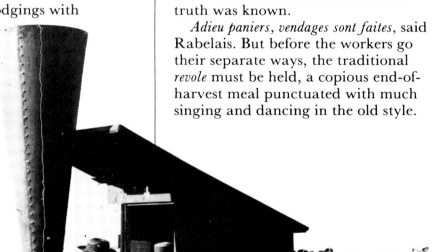

complete sanitary facilities for their temporary guests.

The grape harvest also attracts other less welcome types of worker: tramps, vagrants, down and outs and fugitives from justice wishing to remain anonymous. These characters usually only work for a single day before moving on; they rarely find a job in a proper band of harvesters. Not surprisingly, the *gendarmes* tend to keep a close eye on the vineyards at this period of the year. For example, in the last century a man named David was arrested at Saint-Jean-des-Vignes, who had quietly attached himself to the grape harvesters. He turned out to be one of the celebrated *chauffeurs de la Drôme*, a band of vicious murderers. His fellow workers must have had the cold shivers when the truth was known.

Adieu paniers, vendages sont faites, said Rabelais. But before the workers go their separate ways, the traditional *revole* must be held, a copious end-of-harvest meal punctuated with much singing and dancing in the old style.

Unquestionably, new methods of culture and the evolution of sophisticated machinery have enabled the Beaujolais to change its status from *petit vin de comptoir* to that of a great vintage. But the benefits of machinery can surely be pushed even further. For example, why not mechanize the grape harvest, which is presently so expensive, and causes such difficulties in terms of administrative worries and short-term accommodation for workers?

Well . . . this is a sensitive point. The younger people gaze longingly at the new harvesting machines – not just the wine-growers who are firm converts to mechanization anyway, but also their wives, the cooks, who never seem to have big enough saucepans to feed all those mouths.

So the Beaujolais has been making experiments . . . which so far have been inconclusive. Polite suggestions have been made to manufacturers that machines be adapted to suit the wine-making techniques of the Beaujolais. But at the same time the various heads of viticultural organizations have requested the INAO to publish a decree stipulating that grapes in the Beaujolais should be 'harvested whole', that is, undamaged; a neat twist, which has the effect of prohibiting machine harvesting, without banning it. *Allez Pierrette . . . tu reprendras ta serpette!* In the Beaujolais, the festival of the grape harvest still has every chance of going on for ever.

HEAVEN BOUND

By October's end,
the grapes are in the vat . . .

The vats are ready. All the pipes and recipients have been sterilized. The wine-grower is fully aware that the success of the vinification process chiefly depends on this meticulous pre-harvest work.

At the height of the harvest, the wine-grower metamorphoses into an alchemist, with Beaujolais as his philosopher's stone. It is vital that the grapes arrive in the vats uncrushed, if his wines are to retain their originality – which is why he has rejected the siren call of excessive

mechanization. There's no secret about winemaking in the Beaujolais; you only need to obey the rules.

Nonetheless, the most anxious moment of all comes when the grapes are fermenting in the vats. Twice a day, the wine-grower regulates the fermentation and warms or cools the vats according to the prevalent climatic conditions. Fundamentally, nothing has changed, except that modern equipment is much more trustworthy than the old techniques, which involved listening carefully to the various stages of fermentation and shifting wine from one vat to another to speed (or slow) the process.

The advent of the mustimeter made it possible to choose the correct moment for racking the wine. Formerly, the wine-growers used to wait till the must was no longer covered before racking; this procedure was very rough and ready, even though the old method of judgement by the cupful, *tasse*, has a certain nostalgic appeal.

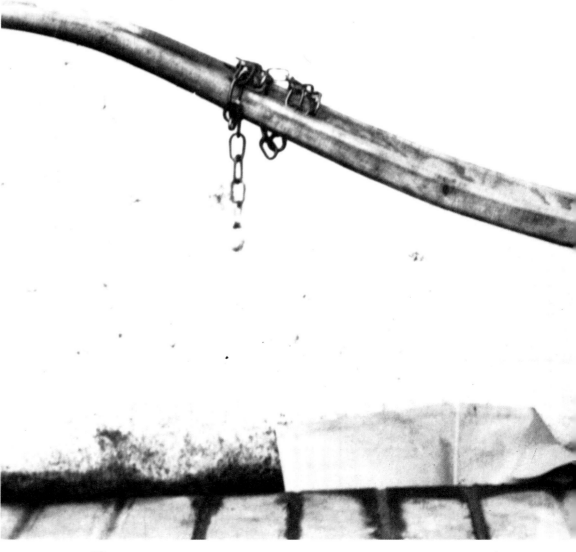

There is no question that the work of technicians and researchers has been very useful in relieving the anxieties of the wine-grower and in greatly improving the quality of the wine. Chaptalization is a technique which has been greatly developed by research and enough nonsense has been said and written about it to fill a book.

The adversaries of chaptalization view it from one angle only: the fact that industrial sugar is added to the must in order to produce more alcohol. Thus, according to them, the wine is denatured. What actually happens is the opposite: chaptalization in the vat, by raising the degree of alcohol, enables tannins and colouring agents to dissolve more readily.

The oenologists, whom nobody can accuse of incompetence, are categorical on this point. . . .

'The addition of sucrose restarts fermentation and contributes to the development of glycerine and other secondary substances produced by fermentation. It contributes to the diminution of acidity by the precipitation of part of the solution of bitartrate of potassium in the wine. Hence chaptalization should not be considered as a practice whose sole purpose is to raise the alcohol content of wine. It improves its savour, by which is meant the impression of body and fullness that it gives.'

I once gave a non-chaptalized Beaujolais to an opponent of the practice. He concluded that the wine was not a Beaujolais at all – and this from a man who liked to boast that he was the equal of many professional tasters and who said he only cared for the Petit Beaujolais of pre-war times. But here let us close this brief technical digression.

The wine-grower goes to his wine-
    press
as a priest goes to his altar.

The first pressing is always a ceremonial occasion. Of course, the old treadmill has vanished, with its husky lads vying to show off their strength to the young maidens waiting for the *paradis* – those first sweet drops which must be caught up instantly and tasted, like the scent of roses, before they vanish. Nowadays, vineyards are equipped with horizontal presses, but the ceremony of the pressing still has its ritual integrity. It embodies the miracle of a safely gathered harvest and the *paradis* opens the doors of ecstasy.

The wine lying in the vat is like a newborn baby in its cradle. It must be jealously cared for and its alcoholic fermentation must be carefully regulated. Ten, sometimes twenty times a day, the wine-grower will go with his *tasse* from one vat to another; his palate infallibly follows the slow transformation of sugar into alcohol and the appearance of the perfumes that are characteristic of Beaujolais. Millions of loyal amateurs all over the world are waiting for this wine. But, before it is delivered up to the greedy hordes, the Beaujolais must do its *malo*, a local term for malolactic fermentation, or conversion of malic acid into lactic acid.

After this, the wine can be submitted to the popular judgement. Each year, it receives its quota of unexpected compliments:

– *Il est coquin, amuseur, un rien espiegle.*
(Cheeky, entertaining, a trifle mischievous.)
– *C'est un polisson, canaille en diable!*
(A scamp, with a wicked twinkle . . .)
– *Ah, mes amis, c'est le petit Jésus qui vous glisse dans le gosier en culottes de velours.*
(Like the baby Jesus, slipping down your gullet in velvet trousers . . .)
– *Et cette robe, regardez cette robe, c'est celle d'une princesse!*
(And look at that colour! fit for a princess . . .)

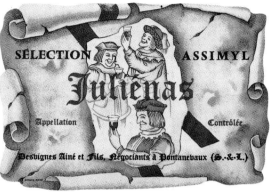

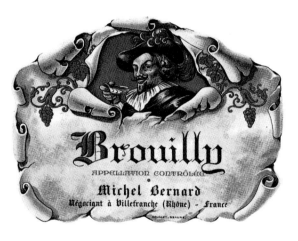

The grape harvest at Saint-Etienne-La-Varenne

Before the tractors came

– *Et quelle grâce!*
(And what charm . . .)
– *Quel parfum! Ça, c'est pas du pathchouli!*
(And what a perfume! No mere patchouli* that!

All these adjectives go out in television, radio and press agency reports, to the great delight of the wine-growers. One pen-pusher even discovered that a certain vintage had the thighs of a Bluebell Girl . . .

But I am inclined to think that Beaujolais, with all the sweat and veneration it inspires, simply has a taste of love.

*Patchouli is a well-known cheap perfume.

HISTORY IS MADE BY MEN

For today's observer, everything seems simple. The wine-grower makes a quality product, the wine-merchant adds the finishing touches, professional organizations arrange for good publicity, the Beaujolais establishes a solid reputation and its solidarity is quoted as an example to other regions. But before this stage was reached, many barriers had to be broken down and many battles had to be won. Many wine-growers, wine-merchants, technicians and ordinary citizens of the Beaujolais fought bitterly for decades to make their region what it is. Their names don't figure in *Who's Who* or the *Almanach de Gotha* and most of them are forgotten. But their work remains; probably this was their sole ambition. Patience and hard work win through! From the eighteenth century

BEAUJOLAIS . . . AND COCA-COLA

Propaganda on behalf of our Beaujolais wines is still a necessity. All our producers are convinced of this. They are not oblivious to the recent inroads made by certain expandable soft drinks from America which are attempting to gain a foothold in French establishments. Compulsive advertising is being carried out on behalf of American Coca-Cola. Trucks plastered with multi-coloured posters have been seen moving along the main arterial road leading across our Beaujolais hillsides. This fizzy water, with one or two additives which give it a bittersweet taste and certain stimulating qualities; this soft drink taken with ice . . . surely, you will say, it cannot seriously compete with our pots de Beaujolais! *But beware! We are talking about advertising and modern trends! Even the name of Coca-Cola has attractive overtones of fun and gaiety. The product is cheap. It's unlikely to be drunk with a good sausage, a roast chicken, or a well-cooked piece of game. But we should beware of it taking over in our cafés and bistros, where the drinking of Beaujolais, and often of vintage Beaujolais, is still so popular. Cafés and bistros are the most important outlets for our wines. A simple cry of alarm — but let's remember how it was with cocktails, toffee apples and chewing-gun.*

Extract from the *Almanach du Beaujolais*, 1950.

onwards, the wines of the Beaujolais were brought down to the Loire along the Beaujeu–Charlieu road. From Charlieu they were shipped to Paris. Their fame had gone out well beyond the borders of the Lyonnais region, and the men of the Beaujolais combined with their colleagues from other areas to press for recognition of the principle of *appellation d'origine contrôlée*. As the creole proverb goes, '. . . with a little patience, a man can pluck the feathers off eggs.' Wine-growers, as a race, are both patient and tenacious. The twentieth century finally ushered in the era of the *appellation d'origine contrôlée*, with the people of the Beaujolais in the thick of all the negotiations that ensued. The first official texts on the matter sought to protect the *appellation d'origine*, but the law of 1905 did no more than set administrative limits to the vineyard areas. Few people on the spot took much notice of this, since none of the technical aspects of winemaking had

yet been addressed, and the 1905 law was completely ineffectual. Nevertheless, one of its provisions still remains in force: the *Service des Fraudes!* For the following reasons: at the turn of the century, the vineyards were still being rebuilt after the invasion of phylloxera. As an encouragement to production, the government advocated the addition of sugar to the wine on a massive scale. As much as twenty-five gold francs per quintal of sugar were offered as a subsidy. The result was a gold rush. Never was so much jam made in France's winemaking regions as in the early years of the twentieth century. In order to restore the sugar to its original destination, authorities were forced to set up obligatory inspections of vats.

The subsidies disappeared a long time ago, only to be replaced by a tax on the sugar used for chaptalization. But the inspections have outlasted successive new laws and governments, just like the *Service de la Répression des Fraudes . . .* the French administration doesn't surrender its prerogatives easily. In 1919, a new law was passed. This too failed. The boundaries of the 'appellations' were no longer an administrative matter, but a judicial one. However, the true Frenchman is a past master at exploiting legislative loopholes. At that time the wine industry was in crisis. Dearth had been followed by abundance . . . and the government had established taxes on wines, but only on everyday wines: *appellations d'origine* were therefore exempted. Hence the new law did not apply to production norms; it concerned only geographic ones. The result was a sudden proliferation of new *appellations*.

The law had other flaws, even after its amendment in 1927 which specified that both land and vine varieties had to be sanctioned by 'local, honest and consistent' practices. However, the wine-growers were in no haste to obtain judicial definitions of their vine varieties and areas of production. They even tried to hoodwink the magistrates with 'agreement suits', whereby they would bring mutual actions in order to acquire *appellations*. In the Beaujolais, a Chénas wine-grower, M

Méziat, concluded that while the law had many failings, it did at least offer wine producers a means of operating as an entity – no longer in commune-based unions, but under the banner of a single *appellation*. Most of the Chénas wine-growers rallied to Méziat's cause, as did those of Romanèche-Thorins in the neighbouring area of Saône-et-Loire.

'We all have the same granitic, manganese-enriched soil. We all have the same vine variety. So let's unite and sell our wine under the same *appellation*!' Heartfelt words, which met an enthusiastic response. But a name had to be found for the new *appellation* which would not revive old local jealousies. 'Thorins', which designated the wines of Romanèche, was just as unthinkable as 'Chénas'. What to do?

At this point, somebody – unknown to history – looked over at the hilltop crowned by its ancient windmill, a witness to at least three hundred grape harvests. 'How about calling it "Moulin-à-Vent"?' he suggested. And thus the first growth of the Beaujolais was born and subsequently authenticated by a series of judgements and rulings. Moulin-à-Vent arrived ten years before the AOCs; it was not until the decree of July 30, 1935 that *appellations d'origine* finally became *contrôlées*. At the same time a body was created to define, protect and regulate the AOCs – the *Comité National*, which later became the *Institut National des Appellations d'Origine des Vins et Eaux-de-vie* (INAO).

The conditions of production imposed by the 1935 decree eliminated a good number of *appellations* created by the earlier legislation. The idea of regulation also disgusted many wine-growers

VENDANGES EN BEAUJOLAIS

Collection LAMARSALLE, Villefranche

LES VENDANGES. — Les Porteurs.

65

An old-style press

Château de Corcelles
APPELLATION BEAUJOLAIS CONTROLÉE
MIS EN BOUTEILLE AU CHATEAU

CONTENTS
750 ml   CHÂTEAU DE CORCELLES G.F.E. • CORCELLES EN BEAUJOLAIS- 69   PRODUCT OF FRANCE
ALC. BY VOL. 12 %

Domaine de la Pierre

Clos Raclet
MOULIN-A-VENT
APPELLATION MOULIN-A-VENT CONTRÔLÉE   75 cl
PIERRE BRAULT - PROPRIÉTAIRE A ROMANÈCHE-THORINS (S.-&-L.)

MORGON
APPELLATION CONTRÔLÉE
75 cl
VIN DU BEAUJOLAIS
SYNDICAT VITICOLE DE VILLIÉ-MORGON (Rhône)
MIS EN BOUTEILLE PAR LES PRODUCTEURS RÉUNIS

Beaujolais nouveau
APPELLATION BEAUJOLAIS CONTROLÉE

CASTEL FRÈRES. NÉGOCIANTS   A VILLEFRANCHE S/SAONE

70 cl   MISE EN BOUTEILLES DANS LA RÉGION DE PRODUCTION

Les **VENDANGES** — Repas des Vendangeurs

LÉMONON-DUCOTÉ ÉDIT MACON

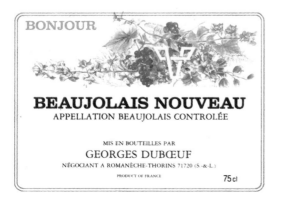

COTE DE BROUILLY

APPELLATION CONTROLÉE

37,5 cl   Sélectionné par Jean Vettard
Restaurateur à Lyon

MIS EN BOUTEILLES PAR
LES VINS GEORGES DUBŒUF A ROMANÈCHE-THORINS (S.-&-L.)
PRODUCE OF FRANCE

Then, after a pause, Papa Bréchard would slyly add: 'He wrote "old blankets" because if he'd mentioned new ones, he'd have had to calculate their depreciation . . .'

LA FÊTE

The Beaujolais wine-growers might agree with Montesquieu, when he says: 'I am in love with friendship.' The wine-grower exports friendship in his bottles; it is rooted in his work, in his vineyard and in the hearts of everyone who lives around him. Friendship is at the core of all the fêtes that take place in the Beaujolais.

The most famous of these is doubtless the *Fête des Conscrits de Villefranche*, held in the administrative capital of the Beaujolais ever since that day in 1850, when two jolly fellows went to the drawing of lots for conscription dressed in opera hats and evening dress. Each year, the young men born between the same dates in a decade parade down the main street of the town. On this occasion the conscripts always show a fine spirit of solidarity, with the wealthier boys taking charge of the poorer ones. This Villefranche custom has overflowed into the surrounding villages of the Beaujolais (though without its originally misogynous character). The *Fête des Conscrits* is the

occasion for a gathering of all generations and families in the village, with singing, dancing and a huge banquet.

In the view of Brillat-Savarin, the destinies of nations depend on the way they eat. In this sense the Beaujolais nation, as we have seen, can boast of its golden destiny. And there are no meetings between folks, no good times, without abundant meals . . . these take place at wine contests, agricultural shows, and on Saint-Vincent's Day, when the wine-growers of most communes still celebrate their patron saint. Nowadays, professional meetings have often replaced the cult of Saint-Vincent in gentlemen's houses, but the meals are still as copious and the wine flows as freely as ever. People also take time to eat especially well on the night before the first of May, when, in a revival of the ancient pagan tradition, young people go from house to house toasting the arrival of the first month without an 'R' in it. Voltaire maintained that since pigs were made to be eaten, men should consume pork all year round. In the Beaujolais, this advice is followed to the letter and a pig-killing is always an excuse for a real party. In the old days, every wine-grower raised his own pig. Today, he relies on the pork butcher, but the *Saint-Cochon* is still ritually observed, with much excitement in the house and a marvellous *fricassée de boudins* shared with the neighbours.

The people of the Beaujolais may be proud and harsh in their working habits, but their greatest joy is to entertain and adopt visitors. Each village has its own fête, but every five years there is a general mobilization for the great *Fêtes du Beaujolais*, which attracts many thousands of visitors from all over the world.

The 'Beaujolais success story' is talked about everywhere. The key to it is perfectly simple, and Gabriel Chevallier, the author of *Clochemerle*, has summed it up to perfection:

'The people of this place see to it that love, harmony and joy prevail over everything, because Beaujolais is a damn good wine which never does any harm. The more you drink of it,

the more delightful you find your wife, the more loyal your friends, the rosier your future and the more bearable mankind. All the evil in the world can be traced to a single fact: that there is only one Beaujolais on the face of the planet. This is the country of the elect and they all have good wine-lover's faces and spirited manners. They offer their hearts in the palms of one hand . . . the hand, that is, that does not hold a glass.'

Pipette *and* tastevin: *two instruments of Beaujolais hospitality*

Charles QUITTANSON

As the proverb goes, *dura lex sed lex*; the law is harsh, but it's the law. Beaujolais submits to the law and is in turn submitted to careful government controls.

The Beaujolais viticultural region produces practically nothing but wines entitled to the AOC label. But what exactly is an *appellation d'origine*?

This ancient idea, which is fundamental in French law, is defined as follows by the law of July 6, 1966, which complements the modified organic law of May 6, 1919, relative to the protection of *appellations d'origine*:

'Shall constitute an *appellation d'origine*, the denomination of a country, area or locality which serves to describe a product originating there and whose quality or characteristics are due to geographic surroundings, including both natural and human factors.'

Hence an *appellation d'origine* qualifies products of quality, whose type and originality are bound to geography (the soil for example), and which owe their specific characteristics to 'natural factors' (such as ground, exposition, altitude, hygrometry, winds, vine varieties, and 'human factors' (vine cultivation, pruning, methods of harvesting and vinification, distillation processes, wine storage methods).

The *appellation controlée* dates from the decree of July 30, 1035, which also created the INAO, a body whose function is to review the rules governing the production of fine wines and brandies, notably on the basis of 'local, honest and consistent' practices. Hence the *appellation controlée* is an evolved form of *appellation d'origine*.

APPELLATIONS D'ORIGINE CONTROLÉE *IN THE BEAUJOLAIS*

There are eleven AOCs in the Beaujolais:

– Regional *appellations*: Beaujolais (and Beaujolais Supérieur), Beaujolais-Villages (and Beaujolais followed by the name of one of the classified communes).
– *Cru appellations* (north to south): Saint-Amour (Saône-et-Loire), Juliénas, Chénas, Moulin-à-Vent, Fleurie, Chiroubles, Morgon, Côte-de-Brouilly, Brouilly (Rhône).
Refer to the table overleaf for the prescribed status of each.

The *appellation* Beaujolais Supérieur can be claimed by the entire area covered by the Beaujolais *appellation*. The *appellation* Beaujolais, followed by the name of a commune, may only be

obtained by a certain number of restrictively designated communes. These are the following:
Rhône: Juliénas, Jullié, Emeringes, Chénas, Fleurie, Chiroubles, Lancié, Villié-Morgon, Lantigné, Beaujeu, Régnié, Durette, Cercié, Quincié, Saint-Lager, Odenas, Charentay, Saint-Etienne-La-Varenne, Vaux, Le Perréon, Saint-Etienne-des-Ouillières, Blacé, Arbuissonnas, Salles, Saint-Julien, Montmelas, Rivolet, Denicé, Les Ardillats, Marchampt, Vauxrenard.
Saône-et-Loire: Leynes, Saint-Armour-Bellevue, La Chapelle-de-Guinchay, Romanèche-Thorins, Pruzilly, Chanes, Saint-Vérand, Saint-Symphorien-d'Ancelles.

These wines can also claim the *appellation* Beaujolais-Villages. The decree of May 6, 1946 opened the right to the *appellation* Bourgogne to wines already possessing a *cru appellation*. In the canton of La Chapelle-de-Guinchay, the principle adopted is the separation of areas giving the right either to the AOC Beaujolais or the AOC Mâcon. The southern boundary of the Mâcon area is confused with the southern boundary of the Saint-Veran area (specifically, two streams, the Arlois and the Préty, are the limits). Hence the communes of Romanèche, La Chapelle, Saint-Symphorien, Saint-Amour and Pruzilly are to be excluded from Mâcon. The assorted red and rosé wines of one of the Beaujolais, Beaujolais Supérieur or Beaujolais-Villages *appellations* may be considered as young wines, *vins de primeur*, and sold for immediate consumption after November 18 of the year of harvest, provided they fulfil the following conditions:
● Volatile acidity below 0.60 g/litre (in H_2SO_4);
● Maximum of 2 g/litre of residual sugar content for red and rosé wines;
● Prior tasting conducted under the aegis of the INAO.

The regulations do not, however, stipulate any time limit for the selling

Le Beaujolais

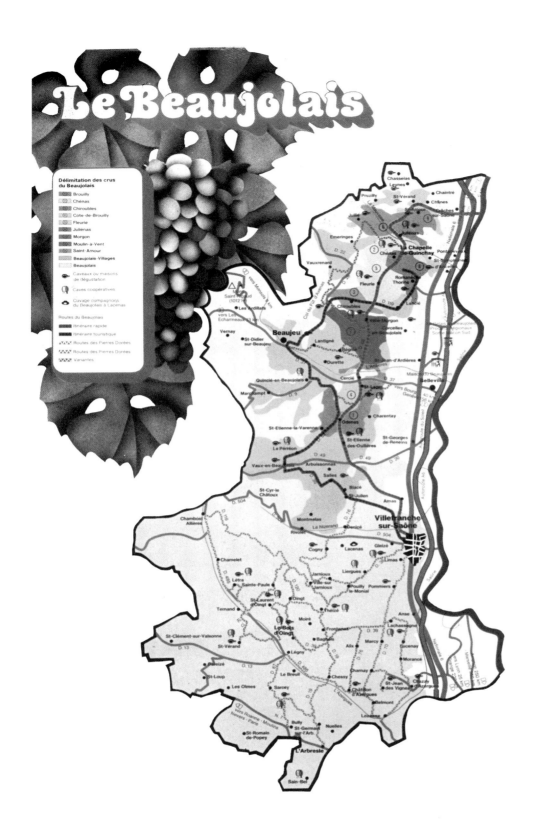

of *vins de primeur*. They should, however, be taken off the market, at the very latest, by the end of the spring following the harvest. This is because their freshness is lost as soon as the warm weather returns.

BEAUJOLAIS VINIFICATION

The following information is taken from an excellent brochure published by the INAO.

Beaujolais vinification may be defined as a vinification of whole grapes which are allowed to macerate for three to seven days. The Beaujolais is the only viticultural region in the world which has preserved this ancestral method, which is often referred to as 'carbonic semi-maceration'. 'Beaujolais vinification' would be more appropriate to describe the superimposition of two phenomena deriving from classic red, *en rouge*, vinification and carbonic maceration. The difference is as follows:

● In a red-pressed vinification, *vinification en rouge foulée*, the wine undergoes a single liquid phase of fermentation. In this form of fermentation, yeasts produce enzymes, causing a series of reactions which ultimately convert sugar into alcohol and secondary substances.

● In a carbonic maceration process, whole grapes are fed into a closed vat which has previously been saturated with carbon dioxide. Thereafter, the wine goes through two parallel phases the liquid phase (the less extensive), consisting of fermenting must derived from grapes crushed during transfer to the vat or by the weight of other grapes; and the solid phase, consisting of the fermentation inside each undamaged grape.

The liquid phase is classic alcoholic fermentation brought about by yeasts; but in the solid phase, a kind of intra-cellular reaction takes place. The cells inside the grape need energy to stay alive. When they have access to air, they acquire this energy by breathing. If the grape is plunged into an airless atmosphere in which oxygen is replaced by carbon dioxide, for a short while it continues to

CHÂTEAU DU PRIEURÉ
BROUILLY
APPELLATION BROUILLY CONTRÔLÉE
SÉLECTIONNÉ ET MIS EN BOUTEILLES PAR
GEORGES DUBŒUF À 71720 ROMANÈCHE-THORINS, FRANCE
PRODUCE OF FRANCE
75 cl

breathe the residual oxygen contained between its tissue cells. When this oxygen has been used up, the metabolism of the grape changes and it seeks to draw life energy from the intra-cellular fermentation of its reserves.

The result is a progressive exhaustion of these reserves and the subsequent death of the grape's cells, which are asphyxiated by residues,

Heavyweight tasting. From left to right: Paul Bocuse, Jean de Saint-Charles, Georges Duboeuf, Pierre Troisgros

LES BRUSSELIONS   750 ML
GRAND VIN   DE BOURGOGNE
Moulin à Vent
APPELLATION MOULIN-A-VENT CONTRÔLÉE
MIS EN BOUTEILLES A LA PROPRIÉTÉ
Jean MORTET - 71570 Romanèche-Thorins (FRANCE)

notably alcohol. This intra-cellular fermentation operates in the absence of micro-organisms (yeast or bacteria). At the end of the intra-cellular process the consistency of the skins alters and they expel all their elements into the pulp. Up to two per cent of alcohol may form in the grape and malic acid may break down in a proportion of thirty to forty per cent, without formation of lactic acid.

Beaujolais vinification also has its liquid and solid phases. The liquid part undergoes classic alcoholic fermentation, and represents ten to twenty per cent of the total volume of material placed in the vat and twenty-five to fifty per cent of what is subsequently taken from it. The solid part is progressively saturated with carbon dioxide by the juice fermenting at the bottom of the vat. Thus there is a more or less advanced intra-cellular fermentation, according to the length of time the wine is left in the vat; but this fermentation never reaches its final stage.

THE WINES OF THE BEAUJOLAIS – AN OUTLINE

We shall confine ourselves here to red wines, since whites and rosés, although distinctive, are still rare in the region.

Beaujolais

The wine known as Beaujolais is mainly produced to the south and west of Villefranche, in the *arrondissement* of Beaujolais. Here the soil is limestone-clay, with occasional sandy patches.

Beaujolais pure and simple is the café wine, *vin de comptoir*, which used to be drunk from heavy forty-five-centilitre bottles, *pots*. It is a vigorous proletarian wine which goes down the throat and out again after the most perfunctory passage through the kidneys. The dominant smells are flowery and fruity; vegetable, rather than animal as in the Pinot Noir wines of the Côte-d'Or. Beaujolais is a wine that must be drunk young, to preserve its freshness and youthful innocence.

CHÂTEAU DE LA GRANDE GRANGE

BEAUJOLAIS-VILLAGES
APPELLATION BEAUJOLAIS-VILLAGES CONTRÔLÉE

37,5 cl

MIS EN BOUTEILLES AU CHÂTEAU PAR
GEORGES DUBŒUF À 71720 ROMANÈCHE-THORINS, FRANCE
PRODUCE OF FRANCE

beaujolais 1970
appellation contrôlée

spécialement choisi pour vous par
la grande cuisine française

mis en bouteilles par
georges dubœuf à romanèche-thorins - 71

Les Sommeliers Parisiens à la Grange. ch

BEAUJOLAIS-VILLAGES
APPELLATION CONTROLÉE
SÉLECTIONNÉ ET MIS EN BOUTEILLES EN EXCLUSIVITÉ
POUR FAG DISTRIBUTION PAR QUINSON et FILS

LA VIEILLE CUVE DU PÈRE PALLANCHER

69820 FLEURIE RHONE FRANCE 75 cl
PRODUCE OF FRANCE

Côte de Brouilly
Appellation Contrôlée
75 cl

QUINSON FILS
NÉGOCIANT-ÉLEVEUR A FLEURIE (RHONE) - FRANCE
PRODUCE OF FRANCE

n -Régnié- *Le 10 Août 1926*

Beaujolais-Villages

Beaujolais-Villages comes from granitic soils, like the region's *crus*. The vine variety is the clear-juiced black Gamay, as elsewhere. The red-juiced black Gamay is forbidden in the area, since it would add an element of vulgarity and an unwelcome dark colour to the wine. Beaujolais-Villages is generally full, but sufficiently robust to keep in bottles for one or two years. It has a more distinctive smell than simple Beaujolais, and has a larger taste due to its firm body.

The Nine *Crus*

The nine *crus* of the Beaujolais are great rivals. Which of them is the best? Like the poet, we say: 'One may as well try to choose between nine pretty girls. Better make love to all of them!'

Saint-Amour

The northernmost *cru* of the Beaujolais, popularized by Louis Dailly.
– Area: 275 hectares. Average production: 13,000 hectolitres.
– Full-blooded wine, known for lightness and voluptuousness rather than finesse. Ages well, but only for a relatively short period.
– Dominant odour: peach, apricot, peony.

Juliénas

This wine was rediscovered by the *Canard Enchaîné* fifty years ago. There is a proverb which maintains 'One should never trust a man who drinks his Juliénas in one swallow'.
– The soil of Juliénas, in the canton of Beaujeu, is generally loamy.
– Area: 560 hectares. Average production: 25,000 hectolitres.
– Solid, firm, nervy at the end of the season. Ages well, though the Juliénas of Jullié and Emeringes tends to be more precocious.
– Dominant aromas: red fruits like cherry, raspberry, blood-peach.

Chénas

The soil is granitic, manganese-rich and salmon-pink in colour. Part of the commune of Chénas is included in

the Moulin-à-Vent area.
– Area: 270 hectares. Average production: 12,000 hectolitres.
– More aroma than Juliénas. Spicy, generous, warm and firm, though refined. The wine has a tender quality which becomes more pronounced on the La Chapelle-de-Guinchay side.
– Dominant aroma: peony.

Moulin-à-Vent

The vineyard surrounds the famous windmill which dominates the landscape. (There is no village of Moulin-à-Vent.) The two communes which produce Moulin-à-Vent are Chénas and Romanèche-Thorins, a straggling village in which the first exhibition of Beaujolais Nouveau is held annually (known as the *Fête Raclet*). The soil is a manganese-bearing, disintegrated granite (known as *gore*).
– Area: 780 hectares; average production: 35,000 hectolitres.
– A serious and vital (*racé*) wine, which ages very well; reminiscent of the great Côte-d'Or Burgundies. Robust and generous, strong colour.
– Dominant aromas: violets and (especially) iris.

Fleurie

The excellent reputation of this *cru* has been carefully nourished by Marguerite Chabert, president of the Fleurie Cooperative and a great character in the annals of the Beaujolais.
– Area: 780 hectares. Average production: 40,000 hectolitres.
– A lady's wine, refined and silky. Fleurie is also light in body; but is not for keeping too long.
– Dominant aromas: amber, iris, above all violets.

Chiroubles

The village of Chiroubles, nestling in its bowl of granitic soil, is famous for the exploit of one of its people, Victor Pulliat, who, in 1888, perfected the technique of grafting on to American rootstock, thereby saving the vines of France. Chiroubles has its own natural terrace, from which the entire Beaujolais may be seen; and its *cru* is the youngest of the region's wines.
– Area: 345 hectares. Average production: 13,000 hectolitres.
– A full-bodied, fruity, distinctive and tender wine.
– Dominant aromas: violets, iris, mignonette.

Morgon

The vines of this *cru* surround the commune of Villié-Morgon. The soils here are unusual, being composed of broken pyritic shale. This is known as disintegrated rock, *roche pourrie*.
– Area: 1000 hectares. Average production: 50,000 hectolitres.
– The wine of Morgon is substantial and generous, with a dark garnet-red colour and a characteristic taste. It ages well.
– Dominant aromas: kirsch, cherry, quince.

Tasse *belonging to Léon Foillard, founder of the* Compagnons du Beaujolais

89

Côte-de-Brouilly

The vineyards of Côte-de-Brouilly stand on the slopes of Mont Brouilly (300 metres), which dominates the region. The soil contains volcanic sand.
– Area: 310 hectares. Average production: 9000 hectolitres.
– A garnet-red wine, substantial, full flavoured, warm and very fruity. Ages well, although its fruitiness tends to fade with time and is replaced by other properties.

Brouilly

The wines of the Brouilly *appellation* grow along the foothills of the Côte de Brouilly, on porphyritic soil. The reputation of this *cru* rests largely on the work of Claude Geoffray, one of the leaders of the movement to establish *appellations d'origine*.
– Area: 1125 hectares. Average production: 45,000 hectolitres.
– Wines to be drunk young; their effect is one of 'inner delight'. Fruity, flavour of fresh grapes.

Beaujolais Primeur

This wine is something apart; every year between one-third and a half of the harvest is drained off in the form of young wine. Beaujolais Primeur is the high-coloured, puppyish, stammering, yet delightful precursor of the maturer Beaujolais to come.

Beaujolais Nouveau sings a song of its own. Its colours are those of the harlequin; red, shining, clear as dawn, shimmering like a rainbow, flowing like spring water.

Beaujolais Nouveau has diabolical charm. It enraptures the drinker, despite its lightness. But, perhaps the last word should be left to René Fallet, who wrote in his famous novel:

. . . And the Beaujolais Nouveau arrived.
And from the North to the Midi, as on every 18th of November of every year, a springtime of little sky blue, red, orange and green posters flowered in the wineshops, announcing to gloomy passers-by that the infant Jesus of wines was born. And the gloomy passers-by brightened at the sight of these leaflets and a droplet of ruby fell into their grey lives, and clung like red confetti to their lips.

AOC	Production varieties			Minimum alcometric level before enrichment and after fermentation			Basic yield per hectare in production		This wine may also be given the *appellation*
	VR	Vr	VB	VR	Vr	VB	VR + Vr	VB	
For all AOCs	Authorised 15% maximum proportion of white vines in red or rosé wines			Degree acquired and potential					
Beaujolais	G, P	G, P	G, Pb, A	9 %	9 %	9,5 %	55 hl	55 hl	BGO
Beaujolais supérieur	»	»	»	10 %	10 %	10,5 %	55 hl	55 hl	Bjs, BGO
Beaujolais + nom commune d'origine	»	»	»	10 %	10 %	10,5 %	50 hl	55 hl	BS, Bjs, BGO
Beaujolais-Villages	»	»	»	10 %	10 %	10,5 %	50 hl	55 hl	BS, Bjs, BGO
Saint-Amour	G			10 %			48 hl		Bjs Or, BV, BS, Bjs, Bgne, BGO
Saint-Amour + nom climat d'origine	G			11 %			48 hl		Saint-Amour, Bjs Or, BV, BS, Bjs, Bgne. BGO
Juliénas	G			10 %			48 hl		Bjs Or, BV, BS, Bjs, Bgne, BGO
Juliénas + nom climat d'origine	G			11 %			48 hl		Juliénas, Bjs Or, BS, BV, Bjs, Bgne, BGO
Chénas	G			10 %			48 hl		Bjs Or, BV, BS, Bjs, Bgne, BGO
Chénas + nom climat d'origine	G			11 %			48 hl		Chénas, Bjs Or, BV, BS, Bjs, Bgne, BGO
Moulin-à-Vent	G			10 %			48 hl		Bjs Or, BV, BS, Bjs, Bgne, BGO
Moulin-à-Vent + nom climat d'origine	G			11 %			48 hl		Moulin-à-Vent, Bjs Or, BV, BS, Bjs, Bgne, BGO
Fleurie	G			10 %			48 hl		Bjs Or, BV, BS, Bjs, Bgne, BGO
Fleurie + nom climat d'origine	G			11 %			48 hl		Fleurie, Bjs Or, BV, BS, Bjs, Bgne, BGO
Chiroubles	G			10 %			48 hl		Bjs Or, BV, BS, Bjs, Bgne, BGO
Chiroubles + nom climat d'origine	G			11 %			48 hl		Chiroubles, Bjs Or, BV, BS, Bjs, Bgne, BGO
Morgon	G			10 %			48 hl		Bjs Or, BV, BS, Bjs, Bgne, BGO
Morgon + nom climat d'origine	G			11 %			48 hl		Morgon, Bjs Or, BV, BS, Bjs, Bgne, BGO
Côte-de-Brouilly	G, P			10,5 %			48 hl		Bjs Or, BV, BS, Bjs. Bgne, BGO, non en Brouilly
Côte-de-Brouilly + nom climat d'origine	G, P			11 %			48 hl		Côte-de-Brouilly, Bjs Or, BV, BS, Bjs, Bgne, BGO, non en Brouilly
Brouilly	G			10 %			48 hl		Bjs Or, BV, BS, Bjs, Bgne, BGO

Nom climat d'origine = Place of origin
Nom commune d'origine = Commune of origin

- **VR** = Vin Rouge; **Vr** = *Vin Rosé;* **VB**: *Vin Blanc.*
- **G** = Essential variety in red and rosé: clear-juiced Gamay.
- **P** = Authorized varieties: *Pinot Noir, Pinot Gris.*
- **C** = Essential variety for white wine: Chardonnay.
- **Pb** = Authorized variety for white wine: *Pinot Blanc.*
- **A** = Aligoté.

BGO: Bourgogne Grand Ordinaire; **BS**: Beaujolais Supérieur; **BV** = Beaujolais-Villages; **Bgne**: Bourgogne; **Bjs** = Beaujolais; **Bjs Or** = Beaujolais, followed by commune of origin.
- Basic yield may be raised before attaining the limit allowed by the classification.

A Villefranche-sur-Saône, aux établissements Lachize et Reymuet, on vérifie le beaujolais qui sera livré dans les bistrots lyonnais.

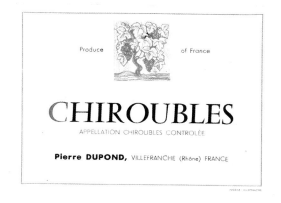

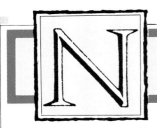

Gaston CHARLE

Just south of Mâcon, the N6 to Lyon skirts one of France's most beautiful vineyard regions: the Beaujolais.

Several million years ago, during the geological convulsions of the Hercynian era, the Massif Central threw up a series of small to medium-sized hills along its eastern fringes. The slopes of these hills are now wholly given over to the cultivation of the vine.

If by chance the passing motorist decides to turn off the N6, or the *autoroute* which runs parallel, to do a little exploring, he will discover the headwaters of the 'third river' so much revered by the people of the Lyonnais region. From the summit of Mont Saint-Rigaud (1012 metres), the eye takes in a vista of 20,000 hectares of vines, bathed in pure sunlight for most of the early spring; a quiet, modest landscape belying a long and eventful history.

Here and there, over a hundred sonorous church towers rise from this ocean of vines. Beyond them stretches the long silver ribbon of the tranquil river Saône, which marks the frontier between Beaujolais and Dombes. Finally, on the horizon, the huge mass of Mont Blanc dominates the high ridges of the distant Alps.

Every year, in these surroundings, the soil of the Beaujolais renders up 1,200,000 hectolitres of wine – 160 million bottles!

DIVERSITY IN UNITY

All the wines of the Beaujolais are made from a single grape variety: the clear-juiced black Gamay. The Gamay is thus the father of the eleven *appellations* of the Beaujolais and of several thousand *cuvées* of infinite diversity every year. But the Gamay was not always the dominant grape of the region.

Today, it is ranked third among all the varieties grown in France, with 50,000 hectares in cultivation (excluding its coloured variations). Philip the Strong's 1395 edict sought to stamp out the '*infame gamay*' altogether, stipulating that all Gamay vines in Burgundy should be uprooted.

Later, the aldermen of Mâcon congratulated themselves on the gift bestowed on them by nature of 'land full suited to producing the best wines for men's health, whilst the Beaujolais can only show wines that are greatly harmful to the human body, since the country thereabouts is only good for Gamay vines, a breed of grape the use of which is forbidden in many places', especially in the county of Burgundy, because it was by nature 'greatly corrosive'.

Three centuries have passed; the Mâconnais has found its proper path, its own variety of vine, and its wine. As to the Gamay, which is the preferred vine for acid soils, it has given Beaujolais an unrivalled reputation as a carafe wine, just as it has spawned a whole range of *crus*, closely related but each with its own character.

But unity goes beyond the grape variety. Technology has developed a single type of vinification for the Beaujolais: the maceration of whole uncrushed grapes with their stalks.

It is at this stage that the influence of man becomes decisive. The lengthening or shortening of the maceration process influences the final constitution of the wine, more especially its degree of suppleness, which in turn affects its aptitude for early consumption or, conversely, the growth of its ageing potential, and thus decides whether it may be sold within a few months, or within a few years, according to the *appellation*.

Moreover, the *Primeur* wines which flood Paris and Lyon (on the third Thursday in November of each year) are no longer contained within the handful of communes which originally built their reputation. Time was when Percheron horses used to go down to the Loire, stopping by Les

Old Beaujolais tastevins
(private collection)

Moulin-à-Vent territory; in the background, Château des Gimarets

Echarmeaux to load the full casks of Beaujolais. The bungs of the casks would be pierced and a straw struck in the hole would allow the small belches of carbonic gas to bubble out of the young wine as it travelled down the road. *Autres temps, autres moeurs.* The unfermented wines of the old days gave way to the *Vin Primeur* which now flows from every corner of the Beaujolais, shaped as it is by the will of the wine-grower. The latter's art, coupled with an appropriate and generally shortened period of fermentation, compensates for the effects – and sometimes the excesses – of any given soil. The wine-grower also accelerates the post-fermentation stages in order to facilitate early bottling, whilst mobilizing the resources of modern oenology to stabilize his product as soon as possible.

The all-powerful client wants his wine to be faultless. It must be limpid, gas-free, reduced to essentials, and innocent of the least sediment. The client must be satisfied as far as possible without allowing mechanical or chemical processes to detract from the wine's originality. Its quality potential and its resources of scent must be preserved, for each Beaujolais possesses its own special perfume from the very first. The oenologist refers to this as 'aroma'; the wine-lover calls it 'fruitiness'.

FRUIT AND FLOWERS

The wines of the Beaujolais are essentially aromatic. The 'fruitiness' contributed by the ripe grape is a fragile and ephemeral quality. This fragility decides the choice of whole-grape vinification, which is the only

Régnié, home of a very fine Beaujolais-Villages

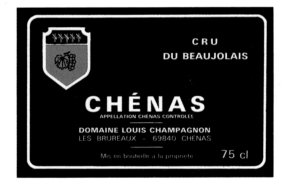

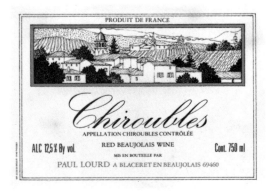

STANCES AU VIN BEAUJOLAIS

O beaujolais, pourquoi l'on t'aime
Tu le sauras assurément
En connaissant nos sentiments
Alors, tu le verras, toi-même,
O beaujolais, pourquoi l'on t'aime...

Tout d'abord, c'est notre œil qui t'aime
Pour ta couleur au teint vermeil
Semblable au rayon de soleil
Qui remplit le cœur tout plein d'ème.
C'est pour ta couleur que l'on t'aime...

Ensuite, c'est le nez qui t'aime
Pour ton parfum fin et discret
Qu'on dirait des fleurs d'un bouquet
Cueilli par le Per'Noé même
C'est pour ton parfum que l'on t'aime.

O beaujolais, pourquoi l'on t'aime,
C'est pour ton fruité savoureux
Qu'on dirait un Nectar des Dieux
Ou bien la Jouvence suprême
C'est pour tout cela que l'on t'aime...

CHANSON COMPOSÉE PAR JULES PETITJEAN
EXTRAIT DE L'*ALMANACH DU BEAUJOLAIS*, 1957

process by which the wine's primary aromatic components can be fixed. The revelation of this aroma is what gives new wine its great charm and its power to delight our tastebuds.

The complexity of aromatic substances, often only found in infinitesimal quantities in the wine, makes them difficult to assess in any qualitative way. Man's olfactive equipment, coupled with a certain amount of training of his sensory memory, is all he has to help him capture these subtleties and nuances. At this point we enter the enchanted garden of wine impressions based on the scents of flowers or fruit, rustic savours, or woodland smells. In the range of Beaujolais wines we are apt to come across the odours of lime-blossom, hawthorn, peach, peony, raspberry, apples, bergamot, cherry, rose, redcurrant, blackcurrant, banana, acid drops – and many others, both simple and complex. All these scents and smells are released by the circular movement of the wine in the glass; they blend and separate in an extraordinary symphony . . . an intricate dance of aromatic cells which sometimes allows one dominant feature to break through, reflecting the soil of the *cru*.

The identification of a *cru* by its dominant odours opens a number of perspectives to specialists in the initial phase of the life of the wine, before oxidation has modified the components of the aroma and turned them into a *bouquet*. Without laying down any hard-and-fast rules, a wine can be recognized through its (usually) dominant aroma. With Morgon, it is cherry; with Chiroubles, violets; Brouilly and Côte-de-Brouilly, the smell of fresh grapes, blackcurrants or redcurrants. Moulin-à-Vent and Chénas share a scent of faded roses; Juliénas is like peonies; Fleurie the iris; Saint-Amour the yellow peach; and Beaujolais and the young Beaujolais-Villages the odour of bananas.

SOIL AND CLIMATE

The vineyard soils of the Beaujolais derive from two geological formations, which meet at the level of Villefranche. These are:

– The crystalline massifs of the north, connecting the eastern edge of the Massif Central.
– The secondary formations of the south, which are made up of clay-limestone soils of sedimentary origin.

The soils derived from the ancient massifs are shallow, highly porous, poor and acid; rocky outcrops covered with a few centimetres of meagre soil. Each time this earth is swept down the hill by storms, men have tirelessly carried it up again. The parcels of ground are often surrounded by drystone walls, which

bear witness to the courage of the old land-reclaimers and their skill in the use of the crowbar. It is here, in the volcanic granite of these formations, that the Gamay vine yields its best results, in the form of Beaujolais-Villages and *Crus*.

The clay-limestone soil of the south contains stones tinged with yellow by iron oxides, turning golden when exposed to the sun. This is the *pierre dorée* which illuminates the south of the Beaujolais and its fine old houses. These colder, deeper, richer soils provide the basic Beaujolais wine, which was often called a bastard wine but now bears comparison with the very best.

The climate of the Beaujolais is generally temperate, though there are extremes of temperature. But since we are talking about vines, more importance should be attached to microclimatic conditions than to regional approximations. Firstly, the hills of the Beaujolais are sheltered by a screen of hills from the cold, wet winds that sweep up the Loire valley, often bringing stormy weather. Secondly, the vines grow on east-facing slopes which look out across the Saône basin. The Saône plays its part in regulating local temperatures, whilst the light that fills its broad plain favours the assimilation of chlorophyll in the ripening grapes. Lastly, the moderate altitude of the vineyards, combined with a gradient steep enough to allow satisfactory drainage, provides the right conditions for the cultivation of quality vines.

FAVOURABLE DEVELOPMENTS

The Beaujolais wine area was originally divided into two zones: Beaujolais and *appellations locales*. From the beginning, the legal arrangements carried the seeds for a third family, which is now well known under the name of Beaujolais-Villages. The Beaujolais production area, which covers 9,600 hectares, lies to the south and west of Villefranche, between the Nizerand and Azergues rivers in the Villefranche district, with a small abutment into five communes of the Lyon district. The *Pierres Dorées* road leads into the heart of the regional *appellation*, which is mostly on clay-limestone, with occasional strips of sandy and granitic soil. The erosion caused by rain adds to this mixture.

The wine-grower of the southern Beaujolais, who for centuries was half farmer, half wine-grower, did not always make the best use of his vines. His vinification methods left much to be desired and the wine often acquired an excessive and unpleasant taste from the earth. The receptacles he used, which were almost exclusively made of wood, tended to deteriorate; they were difficult to repair or replace, with barrel-makers becoming more and more rare.

The problem changed, however,

with the development of oenology and the creation of the first cooperative wineries in 1929–30. Today there are eighteen cooperatives in the region, which handle the vinification of one-third of the total production of the Beaujolais. Their equipment, rudimentary at first, is now thoroughly modern: stainless-steel vats have supplanted concrete ones, allowing the winemakers to achieve complete mastery of temperatures by the manipulation of thermo-regulated systems. The filling and emptying of vats, the transportation of the harvest and the pressing of the grapes is mechanized to the ultimate degree commensurate with a proper respect for the standards imposed by the production of vintage wines.

Today, the wine-grower of the Bas Beaujolais is exclusively a wine-grower. He uses sound vinification methods and produces firmer, slower-developing wines than those of the granitic soils, which acquire all their graces by Easter after the cold winter weather. Once they have shed their original minerality, they exhale a solid, fresh, sappy aroma and their violet-facetted, ruby colour reflects their geological origins. Each year the Beaujolais *appellation* gains ground on the market for new wines, which was once the preserve of Beaujolais-Villages. Created on April 21, 1950, through an administrative simplification of thirty-nine communes and forty-one belltowers (!), Beaujolais-Villages is annually delivered *en primeur* from the end of November onwards. It is light, mischievous and thoroughly drinkable. It is a kind of bridge between the Beaujolais wines discussed above, and the local and commune *cru appellations*. The commercial success of Beaujolais-Villages has never been in doubt since the moment it was created as an *appellation*. The wine trade can count on annual reserves of 300,000 hectolitres, for a total area of over 6200 hectares. In addition, Beaujolais-Villages is something of a technical success story, since to the fifty per cent of regional harvest which leaves the Beaujolais each year it contributes a large proportion. But

let us now move on to a discussion of the *crus*, which are the area's unquestioned ornament.

BROUILLY AND CÔTE-DE-BROUILLY

Quel est donc ce sommet . . .
le bon vin de Brouilly.

These lines by Emile de Villié introduce us to the twin brothers of the Beaujolais family – Brouilly and Côte-de-Brouilly.

From Brouilly to Saint-Amour stretches a sea of short-pruned Gamay vines, ten thousand plants to the hectare, lavishly cared for all through the year. These gnarled and twisted vine stocks have succeeded in pushing their roots into a rock so hard that it successfully resisted the steel implements of quarrymen sent, not long ago, to open up the side of the hill. Mont Brouilly has resisted – and still resists – the onslaught of the centuries, due to the robust nature of its granite and blue-black shale. Mont Brouilly is 485 metres high and stands in the middle of the vineyards, crowned with a chapel built in 1865 and dedicated to Notre-Dame de Fourvières, said to protect the vines against mildew. From the bedroom window in his fine house at Saint-Julien, Claude Bernard saw this chapel being raised and referred to it in a letter to a friend.

Brouilly's vineyards and wines are frequently mentioned and described by authors of former times. Julien, in his 1816 topography of known vineyards, praised the quality of the wines of Odenas and Saint-Lager. In 1857, M Rendu, Inspector-General of Agriculture, situated the 'genuine' Brouilly on the side of Mont Brouilly and called the wine from the area from beyond 'a bastard Brouilly', *Brouilly bâtard*. Nearer our own time, Léon Foillard shows a tendency to place the Brouilly *cru* within the same boundaries and is confirmed in this by different Beaujolais classifications appearing in 1865, 1874, 1891, 1893 . . .

Nonetheless, today's Brouilly *appellation* extends well beyond the limits designated by ancient usage. Let there be no mistake; we do not wish to reignite the quarrel of forty

years ago, which opposed supporters of a purist delineation for the *appellation*, and those – visionaries and opportunists – who preached the extension of Brouilly to include the alluvial soils of its eastern boundary.

Maps dating back to before the tenth century show that place-names ending in *-iacum* were later changed by French into *ié* endings. Thus

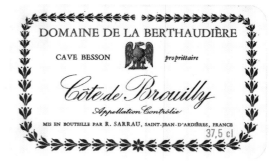

Brulliacum must have become 'Brouillé', not 'Brouilly'. From *brouillé* to *brouille* (quarrel) is only a short step . . .

So we shall confine ourselves to explaining how it is that two *appellations* coexist around Mont Brouilly, without being confused. Both were defined by a decree of October 19, 1938, given their own status, and provided with similar conditions of production. The only difference lies in their geographic location, which for Côtes-de-Brouilly is limited to the slopes of Mont Brouilly and the four communes of Odenas, Saint-Lager, Cercié and Quincié – a total of slightly more than 300 hectares. The present delineation represents the old guard's ideal of a 'Brouilly' appellation. As to straight Brouilly, its preserve covers some of the communes of Mont Brouilly, plus those of Charentay and Saint-Etienne-La-Varenne. Its annual production exceeds 40,000 hectolitres as against 8000 for the Côte. According to a report for the years 1926–34, the total quantity of wine made on Mont Brouilly remained fairly constant, varying between 8000 and 9000 hectolitres. This represents the volume declared at present for the AOC Côte-de-Brouilly. Hence, the extension of 'real' Brouilly required the integration of very diverse soils, ranging from dry granitic to heavy alluvial earth adjoining the plain of the Saône. One readily understands the regrets of those who defended the Côte, like Claude Geoffray – another type of Robespierre likewise defeated by La Plaine.*

At the very heart of the *appellation*, the wines of Côte-de-Brouilly are highly coloured, vigorous, full bodied, and firm. The schistic clay soil bequeaths them their ability (rare in the Beaujolais) to improve with age. The granitic sectors take precedence, producing an increasingly popular table wine. On the edges of the *appellation*, the choices are harder; but both professionals and amateurs will prefer to make their own discoveries and draw their own conclusions . . .

The abundance of *Brouilly* wines ensures them the favour of the wine market, despite their diversity. The

The Madonna of Fleurie. (Painting by G. Cabannes, private collection)

Côte wines, whose characteristics have remained more pronounced and consistent over the years, are less attractive to the industry and often end their careers under their fallback *appellation* of 'Bourgogne'. This is a shame, since they have qualities which should interest a market that is always looking for reliable wine, good for drinking young, but also for keeping. Nonetheless, the Brouilly region preserves a unity which is symbolized by a tasting-cellar at Saint-Lager which is called Cuvage de Brouilly, and much frequented by those lovers of wine and nature who visit the region each year. From the plain to the top of Mont Brouilly, the landscape is studded with beauty spots, *châteaux*, and cool, deep cellars – with names like La Chize, Les Tours, Château-Thivin, Pierreux . . . and during the grape harvest, the hill resembles one great vat, fragrant with the scent of grapes.

*During the French Revolution, La Plaine was a term used to define the moderates in the National Convention who brought down Robespierre.

CHIROUBLES

When the appearance of the dreaded greenfly, *puceron*, was reported for the first time in 1865 at Roquemaure, in the Gard, Victor Pulliat had already been living thirty-eight years at Chiroubles, in the heart of the Beaujolais.

The name of Victor Pulliat features with those of Millardet, Foex, Viala, Ravaz and Planchon as one of those

scientists who saved the vineyards of France from total destruction by phylloxera. Pulliat played his part first on a local, then a worldwide stage. At his domaine of Temperé, he assembled a collection of over two thousand vine varieties, from the study of which he established a scale of precocity which is still a basic reference for all ampelographers. On his death in 1896, he was probably unaware that the village of his birth would one day carry the reputation of its wine far beyond the borders of the Beaujolais.

Chiroubles, nestling in its granite amphitheatre, at 400 metres altitude, is the first communal entity we encounter in our review of the Beaujolais. The village is built closely around a twelfth-century church, as if to leave as much room as possible for the vineyards which crowd in on it from every quarter. It marks the centre of an area that climbs westward to the slopes of Mont Avenas (700 metres).

Just as the vines of Chiroubles belong to a single variety, so the soil of the commune is of a single type: the coarse granite of the Massif de

Fleurie, with occasional patches of granulite earth. The rock, under the combined assault of man and weather, has been gradually worn away, leaving a meagre sandy topsoil which is only good for vines.

The geometrical parcels of land here are separated by ancient walls, built of stones prised out of the ground with iron bars by generations of men.

Along these steep slopes punctuated by sheer drops, the motorized winch is the ideal implement for bringing up both trenching ploughs and the soil, which is often washed off the bare rock by storms.

Light, thin, acid and porous, the soil of the Chiroubles vineyards fulfils all the conditions required to produce quality wines within the territorial limits fixed by the decree of September 11, 1936, which defines the *appellation contrôlée* Chiroubles.

While official recognition did not immediately lead to popular consecration, the merits of the commune's wines were far from unknown to local dealers. We possess a list of tariffs dated December 30, 1879, on which the wines of Chiroubles are priced according to their vintage:

	1874	1876	1877	1878
	(Francs)			
First choice	300	185	135	140
Second choice	280	160	125	120–135

These are prices for two hundred and fifteen-litre casks. By way of comparison, the same vintages from Moulin-à-Vent were sold at 360, 230, 160, 180 francs. Thus Chiroubles was already competing favourably with the *cru* which is generally considered to be the best in the Beaujolais. Certain authors have seen in Chiroubles the intermediate wine – or link – between Fleurie and Morgon. Chiroubles, it is said, has Fleurie's charm and Morgon's solidity. In fact, the qualities of Chiroubles are uniquely its own, even though on the edges of the commune bordering Fleurie, or other *appellations*, these qualities can be confused. At its heart,

it is completely distinctive.

The first visitors to the Maison des Beaujolais were immediately impressed with Chiroubles and from the very beginning it ranked first in the approval ratings of all the *appellations* offered for tasting. We do not know if this is still the case, but at all events, its early success has contributed to the *appellation*'s subsequent vigour.

On July 14, 1953, the Terrasse des Chiroubles was inaugurated on the Fût d'Avenas, complete with an orientation table and the blessing of local officials. The craze for publicity had begun to affect the vineyards and Chiroubles followed Villié Morgon as a pioneer in the field, showing how goodwill could triumph against all obstacles (including lack of money).

Since then, Chiroubles has come a long way. From the communal chalet built in 1958, the visitor can view practically all the 345 hectares of the *appellation*, which produce an average of 13,000 hectolitres of wine each year. The cooperative winery also possesses its own tasting-cellar, so all in all, the *cru* has a particularly strong marketing infrastructure.

It is a fact that Chiroubles, with its elegance, finesse, and scent of violets, is best drunk young – despite declarations to the contrary by oenologists. The very nature of the soil lends itself to the creation of wines with a rich, flowery aroma, short on tannin and colour and drinkable soon after the harvest. There are some *cuvées* which may be kept longer; these are either left to ferment longer in the vat or come from the higher vineyards. Served cool, Chiroubles can be served from the beginning to the end of a meal; as they say, it 'slips down the throat like Jesus in velvet trousers'.

FLEURIE

In 1722, a deputy from the Mâconnais to the States-General of Burgundy declared that the share of the Beaujolais wine production sent up to Paris should be limited to two or three superior *crus*: those of Chénas, Fleurie and Saint-Lager. Thus Fleurie's viticultural antecedents are old indeed.

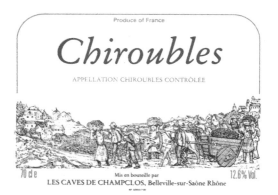

PALAIS DU COMMERCE

MAISON HENRI IV

BANQUET DU 11 JUIN 1911

CAILLES LUCULLUS
SAUMON BRAISÉ Sᶜᵉ NANTUA
SELLE DE PRÉ SALÉ PARISIENNE
CÈPES BORDELAISE
PINTADONS TRUFFÉS
PATÉ DE STRASBOURG
ASPERGES EN BRANCHES

✻✻✻

GLACE PLOMBIÈRES

DESSERT

✻✻
✻

VINS

✻

CHÊNAS EN CARAFES
CHATEAU LA TOUR BLANCHE
CHATEAU CITRAN
POMMARD
WHITE-STAR
✻

Servi par
WATTEBLED & Cᵉ

FONTAINE BARTHOLDI

Imp. B. Arnaud Lyon Paris

emptied his pannier of grapes. The commune is made up of several small hamlets, each with different soils, though all are more or less granitic.

As we have seen, the wine-growers of Chénas were at the origin of Moulin-à-Vent. Thus Chénas has the distinction of possessing two *crus* on its territory, its own, and that of Moulin-à-Vent. Though not related, the two *crus* remain allies, the more so since Chénas flirts with the Saône-et-Loire by extending its *appellation* area across the best slopes of La Chapelle-de-Guinchay. It is said of Chénas that it is 'a bunch of flowers in a velvet basket'. Real lovers of distinctive Beaujolais revere this celebratory wine, which has many points of similarity with Burgundy and was said to have honoured the table of Louis XIII. Because of its modesty and discretion, Chénas probably does not occupy its rightful place in the hierarchy of Beaujolais *appellations*. Perhaps this is because its production area is so limited.

The Chénas tasting-cellar, which stands beside the Route du Beaujolais, possesses a number of historic treasures. It has the intimate atmosphere of a typical local village; and it was once administrated by M Le Haute (former chief tax official of the Beaujolais) who bequeathed to the cooperative of Chénas the finest vaulted cellars in the region.

JULIÉNAS

Juliénas, at the northernmost point of the Beaujolais, stands astride the

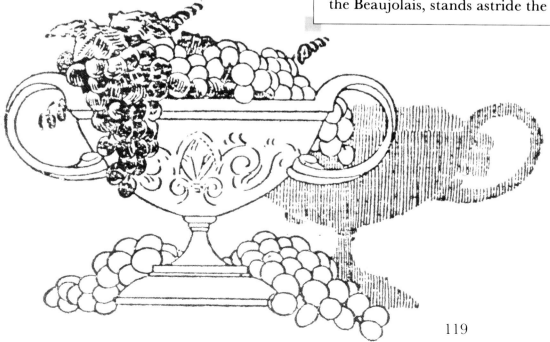

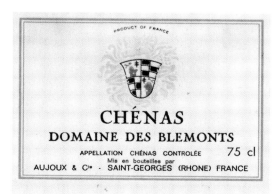

place where Gamay vines end and Chardonnays begin. This choice – and adaptation – of varieties which differ both in colour and disposition, may be explained by the prevalent geological formations and the nature of the resultant soils.

At Juliénas, granite makes way for second-era formations; ancient alluvial deposits, hence deeper, richer soils. Of course, the change is not an abrupt one, since soil layers do not split like schistic slate. Cultivation and erosion have created a smooth blend of earth which is particularly suitable for vines. The fame of Juliénas, outside its connections with the newspaper world, may rest on the fact that grapes were growing here when the rest of the Beaujolais was still a forest – a fact attested by many reliable documents. How did vines come to Juliénas before they reached the easternmost slopes of the region? This remains a mystery.

The commune of Juliénas, spelt 'Julliénas' until the end of the nineteenth century, lies within the district of Beaujeu. It became an *appellation controlée* by a decree of March 11, 1938. The area delimited covers four communes, with an incursion into the Saône-et-Loire. At first, the total AOC area covered 530 hectares 96 ares 99 centiares (note the precision), with 436 h 05 a 38 ca at Juliénas; 2 h 18 a 05 ca at Emeringues; 67 h 84 a 96 ca at Jullié; and 24 h 88a 60 ca at Pruzilly. Since then, certain complementary surveys have increased this area to a little

over 560 hectares. Because they are so close to the clay soils of the Mâconnais, the vineyards of Juliénas give to their wines a deep, intense, ruby colour and plenty of dry matter. This allows them to age very well in certain vintages.

Wines from Jullié and Emeringues are probably less suitable for ageing. We say 'probably', because here, as everywhere else in the Beaujolais, the diversity of soils, expositions, altitude and people lead to wide contrasts.

The wine-growers of Juliénas well know how to take advantage of modern oenological methods, whether they make their own wine from their own harvest, or whether they rely on the cooperative cellars (built in 1960).

In 1660, at Bois de la Salle, Mathieu Gayot, Treasurer of France, built a priory which later became the property of the Sieur Charrier, who in turn built the *château* which today contains the cellars of the *grands vins de* Juliénas. We note in passing that at one time Juliénas was dependent on the chapter of Saint-Vincent-lès-Mâcon, which levied the ecclesiastical tithe on the commune: that is, a tenth part of the land tax imposed. The Revolution abolished this tax, and all that remains of it now is a five-galleried house known as Maison de la Dîme, or des Dîmes, containing the strongroom used by the collectors for storing the tax money. As a former fief of the lords of Beaujeu, Juliénas had many chapels and *châteaux*. Among these was the Château de

Juliénas, which has some of the finest old cellars in the Beaujolais. Its present owner, while he is not the seigneur of the Beaujolais, nonetheless presides over the Cellier de la Vielle Eglise, a tasting-cellar set up in 1955 in an unused chapel. The building has been redecorated by a Paris painter, in a style inspired by the surrounding area; thus the chancel is packed with leaping fawns, impassioned nymphs, rubicund Bacchuses and facetious cherubs. These delightful figures are as charming as the wine of Juliénas, and only an idiot or a teetotaller could be shocked by them.

The Cellier was originally founded by Victor Peyret, who died all too young. His memory is preserved by his friends and successors in the form of a prize, given annually to an artist, painter, journalist, writer or designer who has served the cause of Juliénas. The fortunate winner of this prize is presented with one hundred and four bottles of the best *cru*, amid scenes of much gaiety and festivity.

SAINT-AMOUR

At the extreme northern limit of the region lies Saint-Amour, last of the Beaujolais *crus*. The name Saint-Amour is derived from Saint Amateur, a Roman soldier who was converted to Christianity and founded a monastery on a mountain peak overlooking the river Saône. The story of Saint-Amour is similar to those of many other Beaujolais

Domaine de la Maison de la Dîme.
(G. Cabannes, private collection)

A '*VIN NOUVEAU*' CURE AT JULIÉNAS

An historic day . . .

On September 29, Le Canard Enchaîné is received by its friends and loyal readers, the wine-growers of Juliénas. Juliénas! A name to be remembered and put in bottles. As to the wine-growers, they wear their hearts on their sleeves.

Ten o'clock.

Hillsides; warm, welcoming houses; surrounding vines with foliage turning red in the autumn sunshine; and good friends to greet us.

The time spent on formalities is kept to a minimum.

Straight away, we get down to essentials.

'Mind the steps!'

We're in a cellar. Two cellars. Lots of cellars.

'You're at Juliénas!'

Juliénas starts with everything I mentioned above — hillsides welcoming homes, vineleaves turning red; but it ends with a cellar.

The rest is only secondary.

The tour of the cellars follows a careful ritual. First you are shown the lines of casks; then a small recipient is put into your hands.

'There's your tasse*!'*

This is for tasting the wine.

When we have tasted this year's wine, we have to taste last year's, then the year's before, and so on; then a wine which has a particular type of fruitiness, then another which, though it is less fruity than the most fruity, is nonetheless fruitier than the least fruity, then . . .

It's when you come out of the cellar that the warning should be heeded.

'Mind the steps!'

Strange, there seem to be more than before!

From an article by Jules Rivet, *Canard Enchaîné*, Autumn 1934

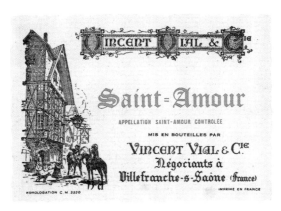

communes. An early prosperity, cut short by the appearance of phylloxera; then wrecked in the years after 1914–18, while the landscape burgeoned with monuments to those killed in the war. The slump in wines in the first years of the century also accelerated a population exodus: a cask cost twenty-five francs at the cooper's, and its contents were worth only twelve francs! Strong arms to wield the mattock or carry the can of sulphate were hard to come by. During the Gallo-Roman era, the people of Saint-Amour numbered around 2000; at the armistice, in 1918, this total had fallen to less than 450.

Today, the population is again on the increase and the status of *appellation contrôlée* has had a lot to do with this phenomenon.

The *Saint-Amour appellation* is the youngest of the nine *crus* of the Beaujolais. It was born in 1946, two years after the others, and it owes everything to the faith and passion of one of its children – Louis Dailly.

The commune lies at the juncture of the granitic zone (with its vocation for fine red wines), and the limestone favoured by the Chardonnay grape. Chardonnay is used to make quality whites such as Mâcon and Saint-Veran. From 275 hectares planted with vines inside the designated area, the average annual wine yield is between 8500 and 9000 hectolitres – all of which goes to satisfy the ever-growing demand for Saint-Amour in France and abroad. The decalcified 'Beaujolais' sector of the *appellation* is made up of clay-silica soils, with clay elements surrounding rocky or pebbly particles which have separated from the granitic bedrock and arkose

(Triassic sandstone). These soils produce highly coloured, solid, substantial wines, which are rich in tannin and may be kept as long as Morgons and Juliénas.

For commercial reasons, and in order to ensure a rapid turnover, some growers here apply *vin nouveau* technology and produce lighter-coloured wines to be drunk young. We believe that they are mistaken and that Saint-Amour, like the other *crus* (with the possible exception of Chiroubles) should confine itself to producing wines for bottling and for the restaurant market.

When properly made and bottled at the right time, Saint-Amours offer all the fruitiness of the Gamay grape, and lose nothing of their distinctiveness. They can always be relied upon as a fit accompaniment to roasts, game and the cheeses of the Beaujolais hills. If anyone needs convincing of the real quality of Saint-Amour, he need only come to taste the selection offered by the Caveau des Saint-Amour, which has operated since 1965 in a converted garage. This building has been completely altered, adapted to tasting needs and decorated by the Lyon-based painter Nicolas Janin with frescoes and scenes of the grape harvest. So nothing has been lost . . . and Saint-Amour hopes soon to expand its *appellation* by a few dozen hectares, the better to satisfy its loyal customers.

The village of Saint-Amour-Bellevue

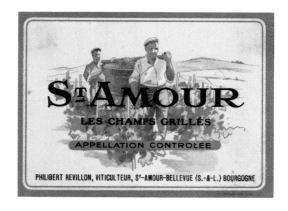

PISSE-VIEILLE

This legend is one of the most popular in the Beaujolais. It has given its name to the famous cru *of the hamlet in the commune of Cercié, and it is told all across the region, with slight variations. Here is one version, translated from the dialect.*

There were once two old people living together and the wife was very pious, often going to confession. One fine day, a new curate was appointed. The old woman said to herself: 'I'll go and see what he's like, I'll go along and confess.'

The old curate had been a fine confessor. How would the new one turn out? Perhaps he didn't speak the dialect very well. When the new curate had given the old woman absolution, he told her:

Allez, et ne pêchez plus! *(Go, and sin no more!) But she understood him to say:*

Allez, et ne pissez plus! *(Go, and piss no more!)*

When she arrived back home, she said:

'Toine, you don't know what he gave me as a penitence: I'm not to piss any more!'

'Well, if that's what he said, you'd better not!' So, of course, she had a terrible night, and the next day was even worse. The poor old woman suffered greatly. Toine went out to tend his vines and by the time he got back at noon, his wife could scarcely stand it. Another day passed, and finally she said:

'Toine, go and find the curate, tell him I can't bear it a moment longer: let him give me a hundred Paters *and a hundred* Aves *if he likes, but not this. He has to let me piss!'*

So Toine went off to the curate, who said:

'I never said that! I never said she shouldn't piss! I told her to sin no more!'

Ah! Toine went galloping home and Toinette his wife was up on the balcony waiting for him. He saw her from a long way off and shouted to her:

'Oh, Toinette! Pisse, vieille! Pisse, vieille! Le curé l'a dit! (Piss, old girl, the curate says you can!)

It happened there were some little boys among the vines nearby, and they heard this and doubled up laughing. And ever after, when they saw the old woman go by, they called out to her, 'Pisse, vieille!', which is how the name has stuck to the village.

VINTAGES

Gaston CHARLE

Nature, who is kind and cruel by turns, and man, who tries to correct her caprices, each year combine their forces to create original wines. From one harvest to the next, wine changes its fundamental characteristics, modifying its evolution, and varying its expectation of life. As evidence of this perpetual diversity, here is a breakdown of Beaujolais vintages over the last twenty-six years.

1960: Despite unfavourable weather, this vintage produced a few good growths; fruity, well coloured, but to be drunk early.

1961: Very good quality. Fine colour, good balance between body and alcoholic content, and fruity flavour – these were the distinctive characteristics of this vintage, which was an immediate commercial success. In the *crus*, as in the south of the Beaujolais, the wines were full, firm and suitable for ageing.

1962: This vintage was generally satisfactory. The *primeurs* were successful in their allotted areas: on granitic soils. Wines from the clay-limestone districts were aggressive for a certain length of time. The '62s were wines of character.

1963: The harvest this year was late, only beginning on October 5. '63s proved to be *primeurs* rather than *vins de garde* (for keeping); they reminded some (nostalgic) people of the wines

of yesteryear, *les petits beaujolais des bistrots lyonnais*.

1964: By contrast with the preceding year, 1964 was exceedingly dry. All the skill of the wine-grower was necessary to obtain a successful result, which came in the form of wines conforming to type in the *crus*. '64s will keep well.

1965: To use a local expression, this was an *année pourrie* (a rotten year), which resulted in carafe-type wines, light and for rapid consumption.

1966: Thanks to a warm autumn which greatly assisted the ripening of the grapes, this year's wines proved to be healthy and drinkable.

1967: This vintage was an all-round year, both for carafe wines, produced in the granitic areas, and for characteristic *crus*. In general, the wines produced were well balanced, supple and full bodied. Their colour was not particularly strong, but the tone of it was a fine cherry-red.

1968: The vintage was much affected by heavy rain. Only the *primeur* wines were constant in quality in this difficult year.

1969: A year that began with a number of problems (few grapes, washing away of pollen by spring rains, hailstorms), 1969 ended by producing quality wines by virtue of a fine autumn. The wines proved well constructed and full bodied. Their colour was brilliant, a gleaming red, and the *crus* were able to make wines for laying down such as had not been seen since 1961.

1970: The 1970 production exceeded one million hectolitres. A healthy harvest, well ripened from the end of September onward, gave very agreeable, well constituted, and well balanced wines. This impression was confirmed by a very active demand for *primeurs*, which for the first time exceeded 100,000 hectolitres.

Beaujolais

APPELLATION CONTROLÉE

75 cl

Mis en bouteille par THORIN F 71570 PONTANEVAUX
Product of France

IMF CLOS DU MOULIN · 01140 THOISSEY

TRADE MARK

Produce of France

Beaujolais

APPELLATION BEAUJOLAIS CONTRÔLÉE

SÉLECTIONNÉ ET MIS EN BOUTEILLES PAR
PAUL SAPIN VINS FINS A LANCIÉ (RHÔNE) FRANCE

75 cl

PAUL SAPIN

LA SEULE MAISON DE BOURGOGNE
AYANT OBTENU LA
GRANDE MEDAILLE TRADITION FRANCE

MAISON FONDÉE EN 1865

GRANDS VINS · DE BOURGOGNE

Chiroubles

APPELLATION CHIROUBLES CONTROLÉE

MOMMESSIN

NÉGOCIANT - ÉLEVEUR A MÂCON (S&L) FRANCE

VIN DE FRANCE

Beaujolais Supérieur

Appellation Beaujolais Supérieur Contrôlée

CHÂTEAU DU GRAND TALANCÉ

Mis en bouteilles au Château pour

J. PELLERIN À SAINT-GEORGES-DE-RENEINS (RHÔNE) FRANCE

75 cl

Château de Nervers
1984

CUVÉE CHOISIE
PAR
PAUL BOCUSE

RESTAURATEUR
À
COLLONGES-AU-MONT-D'OR

Brouilly

APPELLATION BROUILLY CONTROLÉE

MIS EN BOUTEILLE A ROMANECHE-THORINS
PAR LE SAVOUR CLUB, NÉGOCIANT A LANCIÉ, RHÔNE

PRODUCE
OF FRANCE

Savour Club

75 cl

PRODUIT DE FRANCE

CHÂTEAU DE BUSSY

APPELLATION BEAUJOLAIS CONTROLÉE

Beaujolais

mis en bouteille   en région de production

par Joseph VERNAISON   BELLEVILLE 69220 FRANCE

 e 75 cl

L. RUEL POITIERS 82

TRADITION

PRODUCE OF FRANCE

Clochemerle

Beaujolais-Villages

APPELLATION BEAUJOLAIS-VILLAGES CONTRÔLÉE

75 cl

Mis en bouteilles en exclusivité par
MAISON FRANÇOIS PAQUET, NÉGOCIANT-ÉLEVEUR, LE PERRÉON (RHÔNE)
FRANCE

IMP. DURAND-71000

PRODUCE OF FRANCE

DEPUIS 1849

LE PIAT DE BEAUJOLAIS

APPELLATION BEAUJOLAIS CONTRÔLÉE

MIS EN BOUTEILLE PAR PIAT PÈRE & FILS

NÉGOCIANTS-ÉLEVEURS A LA CHAPELLE-DE-GUINCHAY, S.-&-L.

FRANCE

750 ml e

Beaujolais-Villages

APPELLATION CONTRÔLÉE

Domaine de la Sorbière

Mis en bouteille au Domaine

75 cl

S.A.R.L. DES DOMAINES JEAN-CHARLES PIVOT
"LA ROCHE" QUINCIÉ-EN-BEAUJOLAIS - 69430 BEAUJEU FRANCE

Domaine de la Bourdonnière

MORGON
APPELLATION MORGON CONTROLÉE

MIS EN BOUTEILLES PAR

T. DAVID & L. FOILLARD

NÉGOCIANTS A ST-GEORGES-DE-RENEINS (Rhône)

FRANCE

L. WITRANT Propriétaire à Lantignié

e 75 cl

IMP. CLOS DU MOULIN - (01140) THOISSEY

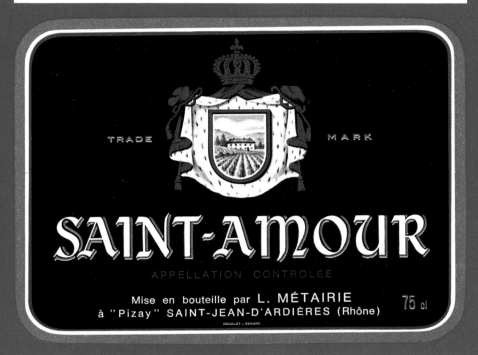

TRADE · MARK

SAINT-AMOUR
APPELLATION CONTROLÉE

Mise en bouteille par L. MÉTAIRIE
à "Pizay" SAINT-JEAN-D'ARDIÈRES (Rhône)

75 cl

PRODUCE   OF FRANCE

BROUILLY
APPELLATION BROUILLY CONTRÔLÉE

AUJOUX

MIS EN BOUTEILLE PAR AUJOUX, A St-GEORGES-DE-RENEINS (69) FRANCE

PRODUIT DE FRANCE

MOULIN A VENT

APPELLATION MOULIN-A-VENT CONTROLÉE

75 cl

MIS EN BOUTEILLES PAR

CHANUT FRÈRES

Négociant-Eleveur à Romanèche-Thorins (Saône-et-Loire) France

Q / 7975 / a

création imp. gougenheim lyon

---

beaujolais n♥uveau

appellation beaujolais
contrôlée

1984
A BOIRE
FRAIS

MIS EN BOUTEILLE EN BEAUJOLAIS
PAR E. LORON ET FILS
A PONTANEVAUX S.L. (FRANCE)

70 cl

PRODUIT DE FRANCE

CHIROUBLES

APPELLATION   CONTRÔLÉE

750 ml

mis en bouteille par

Jacques Dépagneux négociant à Villefranche (Rhône)

G / 24

création imp. gougenheim lyon

Beaujolais-Villages

DEPUIS 1865

Mis en bouteille et choisi pour vous par

Didier Mommessin

MOMMESSIN

75cl

Les Vins Mommessin à La Grange Saint-Pierre - France 71000

GEORGES DUBŒUF

BEAUJOLAIS REGNIE

APPELLATION BEAUJOLAIS REGNIE CONTROLÉE

MIS EN BOUTEILLES PAR
LES VINS GEORGES DUBŒUF
71720 ROMANÈCHE-THORINS

75 cl

PRODUCED AND BOTTLED IN FRANCE

CHIROUBLES

APPELLATION CHIROUBLES CONTROLÉE

75 cl

MIS EN BOUTEILLE PAR

CLUB FRANÇAIS DU VIN   LANCIÉ 69220 FRANCE

DOMAINE BRISSON

APPELLATION MORGON CONTROLÉE

Morgon

mis en bouteille — en région de production
par Joseph-VERNAISON — BELLEVILLE 69220 FRANCE — e 75 cl

L. RUEL POITIERS 82

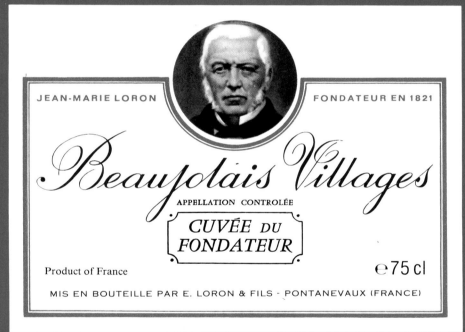

JEAN-MARIE LORON — FONDATEUR EN 1821

Beaujolais Villages

APPELLATION CONTROLÉE

CUVÉE DU FONDATEUR

Product of France — e 75 cl

MIS EN BOUTEILLE PAR E. LORON & FILS - PONTANEVAUX (FRANCE)

"*cuvée de la belle vie*"

PRODUCE OF FRANCE — 75 cl

BEAUJOLAIS-VILLAGES

Appellation Beaujolais-Villages Contrôlée

MIS EN BOUTEILLE A 69820 FLEURIE PAR

QUINSON FILS

IMP. CLOS DU MOULIN 01140 THOISSEY

Mis en bouteilles par
LOUIS TÊTE
St Didier sur Beaujeu, Rhône

Côte de Brouilly

APPELLATION COTE DE BROUILLY CONTROLÉE

70 cl

PRODUCE OF FRANCE

CHATEAU DU PETIT TALANCÉ

BEAUJOLAIS

APPELLATION BEAUJOLAIS CONTROLÉE

MIS EN BOUTEILLES PAR
T. DAVID & L. FOILLARD

FRANCE   NÉGOCIANTS A ST-GEORGES-DE-RENEINS (Rhône)   e 75 cl

Mª CLOS DU MOULIN - 01140 THOISSEY

Jean Lafitte

Produce of France

JULIÉNAS

APPELLATION JULIÉNAS CONTROLÉE

*Je ne connais de sérieux
ici-bas que la culture de
la vigne.* VOLTAIRE

75 cl   *Mis en Bouteille par*

LES CHAIS RÉUNIS A VILLEFRANCHE-SUR-SAÔNE

MOULIN-A-VENT

APPELLATION MOULIN-A-VENT CONTROLÉE

75 cl

Mis en bouteilles par
Albert DAILLY à Romanèche-Thorins (S.-et-L.)

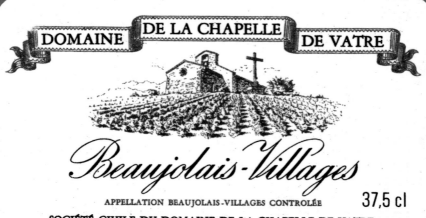

DOMAINE **DE LA CHAPELLE** **DE VATRE**

Beaujolais-Villages

APPELLATION BEAUJOLAIS-VILLAGES CONTROLÉE

37,5 cl

SOCIÉTÉ CIVILE DU DOMAINE DE LA CHAPELLE DE VATRE

MIS EN BOUTEILLE PAR R. SARRAU, SAINT-JEAN-D'ARDIÈRES, RHONE, FRANCE

LA JACQUIÈRE

PRODUCE OF FRANCE ®

BEAUJOLAIS

Appellation Beaujolais Contrôlée

Mis en bouteille par

AUJOUX

750 ml

A SAINT-GEORGES DE RENEINS (RHONE)

CHÂTEAU DE JAVERNAND

CHIROUBLES

APPELLATION CHIROUBLES CONTRÔLÉE

Sélectionné et mis en bouteilles par

GEORGES DUBŒUF NÉGOCIANT A 71720 ROMANÈCHE-THORINS, FRANCE

PRODUCE OF FRANCE

37,5 cl

IMP. MARCHAND 0140 THOISSEY

PRODUCT OF FRANCE

1983

Romanorum Villa in Agro Thorinse (IXᵉ Siècle)

CHÂTEAU DES JACQUES

Moulin-à-Vent

APPELLATION MOULIN-A-VENT CONTROLÉE

75 cl

SOCIÉTÉ CIVILE D'EXPLOITATION DE ROMANÈCHE-THORINS

PROPRIÉTAIRES-RÉCOLTANTS 71570 LA CHAPELLE-DE-GUINCHAY

PRODUIT FRANÇAIS

BROUILLY

APPELLATION BROUILLY CONTROLEE

Domaine de la Folie

Mis en bouteille par J. BEDIN à 69830 BLACERET - FRANCE

RED TABLE WINE ALC. 12,5 % BY VOL. PRODUCT OF FRANCE CONT. : 750 ML

Imported by : *Franche Comté*, Ltd., FAIR LAWN, N.J.

MAISON FONDÉE EN 1865

Moulin à Vent

DOMAINE DE CHAMP DE COUR
APPELLATION MOULIN-A-VENT CONTROLEE

MOMMESSIN

Négociant à la Grange Saint-Pierre, 71000 France

ANNE DE BEAUJEU

BEAUJOLAIS·VILLAGES
APPELLATION BEAUJOLAIS-VILLAGES CONTROLÉE

750 ml  1984

Mis en bouteille par
THOMAS LA CHEVALIÈRE
NÉGOCIANT A BEAUJEU (FRANCE)
Produce of France

№ 14007

"LA ROILETTE"

FLEURIE
APPELLATION FLEURIE CONTROLÉE

MIS EN BOUTEILLE PAR
VINS DESSALLE
69220 SAINT-JEAN-D'ARDIÈRES (RHONE) FRANCE

Red Burgundy Wine	selected & imported by	Contents 750 ml
	Grape Expectations	
Produce of France	emeryville, california	Alcohol 13% Vol.

Pots *of Beaujolais at the station at Lyon*

LA BEAUJOLAISE

Il est en France de doux coteaux,
Où, alignés, vont à l'assaut,
Vrilles au vent, les ceps tordus
Qui sont, au travail, entendus
A puiser au fond de la terre
Du rocher le suc salutaire,
Où l'eau va toute à la rivière,
Où le vin seul emplit les verres.

Aimons le Beaujolais joli
Où la vigne a trouvé son lit,
Aimons le joli Beaujolais
Dont les caves sont les palais.

Il est en France un peuple insigne
Qui a pour maîtresse la vigne;
Son cœur, comme ses pousses, est vert.
Il est rouge, tel son proche hiver,
Aux belles il donne la réplique
Et son âme à la République.
Dur au travail, tendre à l'amie,
D'un pot il régale sa mie.

Chantons le Beaujolais joli,
Tra la li, tra la la, la li
Chantons le joli Beaujolais
Au nom frais comme un ruisselet.

Il est en France un vin fameux
Quand il glisse aux gosiers heureux,
Les yeux reflètent sa malice.
Qu'on se garde bien qu'il vieillisse!
En lui du jour est la chaleur
Et, des belles nuits, la fraîcheur.
A qui le boit tout est aisé,
Il est aux lèvres un long baiser.

Buvons le Beaujolais joli
Qu'il gonfle nos ventres sans pli.
Buvons le joli Beaujolais
Qui nous fait tendre le... mollet.

O Beaujolais, mon bon terroir
Tu es le ciel, sans contredit,
Car, chaque année, de tes pressoirs,
Coule pour tous le paradis.
Aussi aimons, chantons, buvons
Le Beaujolais. Pour lui vivons,
Amis! heureux de ses bienfaits,
Unis dans un accord parfait.

CHANSON COMPOSÉE PAR CATHERIN BUGNARD
EXTRAIT DE L'*ALMANACH DU BEAUJOLAIS*, 1937

by the good offices of President Herriot – but he never did even a drawing of the sluggish Saône. 'I can't do water', he would say to excuse himself; perhaps he was taking an unconscious revenge for the diluting of his Beaujolais. . . .

LE BEAUJOLAIS NOUVEAU EST ARRIVÉ

Beaujolais is the wine of unaffected pleasure; the ultimate party wine. Everyone who has studied it and tried to discover the personality has agreed on one thing: that Beaujolais should be drunk in bumpers, like the joyous thing it is. Also it must be served cool, in glasses filled to the brim – *rouge-bords*, as Boileau-Despreaux has called them, which became *culs-blancs* in a single draught. For years now, from that moment on November 15 when (according to the law which regulates everything, even our hunger and thirst) the Beaujolais of the year can finally be poured into glasses; on that day a party begins which transcends all frontiers. On November 15, all over the world, a cry of delight is heard: *Le Beaujolais Nouveau est arrivé*.

Hundreds of thousands of hectolitres specially vinified for Beaujolais Primeur, leave the region within a few hours on trucks, trains, ships and planes, bound for the five continents of the earth. Beaujolais Nouveau has been brought to Paris by runners and by balloon . . . many of its admirers come to fetch it on the spot and on the night of November 15, the Beaujolais becomes a kind of vinous Babel, in which all tongues blend into an *esperanto* of new wine. Just before Christmas, the news appears in the form of handbills or scrawled in whitewash on bistro windows – a hymn to joy, a challenge to winter. *Le Beaujolais Nouveau est arrivé*, and to hell with the freezing weather. The wine carries the memory of spring smiles and summers gold . . . Thereafter, from Tokyo to Montreal, by way of Sydney, London, and the twin towers of Notre Dame, the consumption of Beaujolais begins in earnest.

There are the straight drinkers, who reminisce about old time bistros, where friends went to lay plans for

changing the world, and to sit around tables covered in red circles from the bottles. There are the couples who go to pledge their love in the same glass of Beaujolais. There are the connoisseurs, who sample the wine as one might tickle a pretty girl, to feel the silkiness of her skin and sense the freshness of her laughter.

And there is that whole crowd of lookers on, gourmands, and seekers of good fellowship, who came up to the red troughs as if they were paying a visit to a well-loved friend, because he is always there to make skies less grey, neighbours more pleasant, wives more bearable, and work less hard. With this extra advantage – according to the old Beaujolais saying – that the wine drunk by men will later do good to women.

THE BENEFITS OF BEAUJOLAIS

Beaujolais is a gift of God to gatherings of friends, to summer evenings spent playing *boules*, or to family reunions. It is no accident that the first official rules and the first written codification of the game of *boules à la Lyonnaise* were worked out in the Beaujolais by Pierre Guillermet.

The priests of the region use the local wine at communion, when it is transmitted by the Eucharist into the blood of Christ. But they also see it as a philtre of smiling wisdom in this region of small wine-growers, where the oldest and most solid virtues still survive: work, patience, generosity, dignity and love of the job well done.

This '*Civilisation Beaujolaise*' is manifested by a certain way of looking at life and adapting to it, without slavish conformism, and

Moulin-à-Vent, *1923. Utrillo's gift to his godson (private collection)*

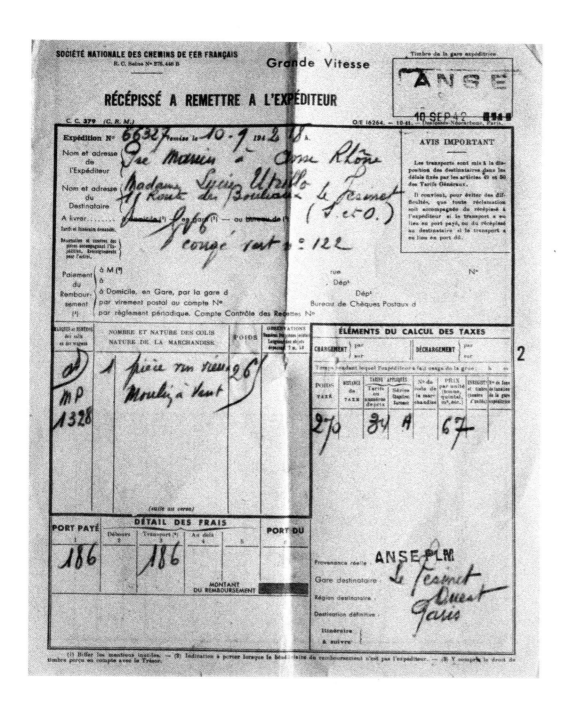

BEAUJOLAIS

Appellation Contrôlée

Cuvée sélectionnée pour Pierre GARAT
par la Jeune Chambre Économique de Belleville

Fleurie

APPELLATION FLEURIE CONTROLÉE

73 cl

DOMAINE DES GRANDES COTES

Stéphane BESSONE
Propriétaire-Récoltant à VAUXRENARD (Rhône)

MIS EN BOUTEILLE A LA PROPRIÉTÉ

St-Didier-sur-Beaujeu, le 14 février 1983

CUVÉE
LANCEMENT

PEUGEOT 205

BEAUJOLAIS-VILLAGES
APPELLATION CONTROLEE

Cuvée Spéciale   Tour de France

BEAUJOLAIS
APPELLATION BEAUJOLAIS CONTROLÉE

0,75 l

UNION INTERPROFESSIONNELLE DES VINS DU BEAUJOLAIS
VILLEFRANCHE (RHONE) FRANCE

BEAUJOLAIS

APPELLATION CONTROLÉE

COMTE B. DE LAGUICHE
PROPRIÉTAIRE A LACHASSAGNE, RHONE

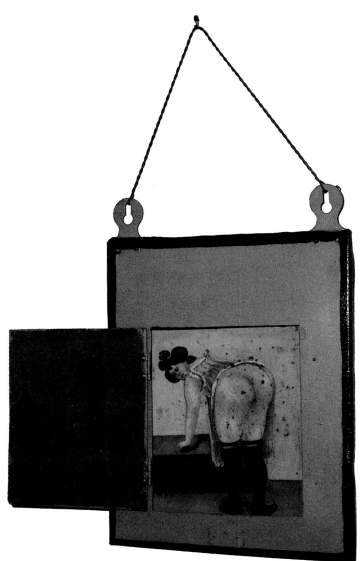

In Boules Lyonnaises, *a very popular game in the Beaujolais, whoever scores no points at all has to kiss 'Fanny' (private collection)*

LA CHANSON DU BEAUJOLAIS

Entre la Cévenne et les Dombes,
Ceinturé d'un ruban d'argent,
Le Beaujolais joyeux s'étend
Avec ses monts avec ses combes.
Au printemps, sous les rayons d'or,
Ses pommiers blancs, ses pêchers roses
Égayent la vigne morose
Qui, paresseuse, dort encor.

Refrain

Oh ! mon joli Beaujolais
Aux sapins verts, aux vignes blondes,
Tes deux aspects je les connais
Les aimant plus que tout au monde.
Sol riche aux flancs généreux,
Ton vin verse l'espérance.
Je te nomme sous ton ciel bleu,
L'un des plus beaux joyaux de France.

II

Dans le temps de la Préhistoire,
Pays tout couvert de forêts
Les fayettes, les loups furets
Se cachaient dans tes combes noires.
Puis, les Romains t'envahissant,
Sur tes flancs, plantèrent la vigne.
Notre sol s'en montra très digne
Et ton bon vin, c'est notre sang.

(Au Refrain)

III

Fait de bons raisins sans mélange,
Ton joli vin c'est un rubis
Rempli des refrains que l'on dit
Au cuvier, les soirs de vendange.
Du vigneron, c'est la fierté.
Du doux poète, c'est la muse.
Mais ce nectar est plein de ruse
Buvons-le sans témérité.

(Au Refrain)

IV

Chère terre toujours féconde
Garde la paix pour ton bonheur.
Reste digne de ton labeur
Ton vin réconfortant le monde.
Il nous faut de robustes bras
Des cœurs vaillants, des âmes fortes
Et sur le seuil de bien des portes,
Je vois encor de nobles gâs.

(Au Refrain)

*Song composed by Zulma Cinquin-Sapin (extract
from* L'Almanach du Beaujolais, *1955)*

without taking things too seriously. Add to this a strong dose of horse sense, gaiety, love of broad jokes, a touch of emotion, earthiness, and the gift of serenity without fatalism.

Take the example of the curate invited to the wedding feast of two of his flock, whose union he had consecrated. With each fresh course that was laid on the table, he raised his glass and exclaimed:

'My Children, with this gift of God, we must drink good Beaujolais wine.' When the dessert arrived, a guest from the City thought it witty to enquire: 'But tell us father, according to you with what should we *not* drink Beaujolais?'
'With water', replied the good curate emptying his glass.

Another story is that of Toine, a small wine-grower who had a wife, Claudine, two goats, a cow, and some chickens. In addition Toine held the post of rural policeman, *garde champêtre*. One day his wife, Claudine, heard him cursing like a trooper down in the stable.
'Toine, whatever's the matter?'
'It's the cow. She won't drink a drop.'
'Well, put your cap on her head. She'll drink all right – more than she can hold.'

And then there is the old Beaujolais saying: 'A woman is like an enema – easier to take than to hold.'

Finally, we would cite the intense

satisfaction derived by the wine-grower from drinking his own wine in his own cool cellar, with its stone pillars and damp sand along the corridors between the lines of barrels – those great casks of 216 litres, each waiting silently for its day.

Though it is a happy wine, Beaujolais also has a way of bringing in a solemn note; for it raises happiness almost to the level of ritual. This is partly the work of the brotherhoods of the Beaujolais, *confréries*. During the course of *Chapitres* or *Tenues*, the *confréries* of the Beaujolais regularly elect new members (provided they have passed certain initiatory tests) from the ranks of neophytes who have been captivated by the juice of the Beaujolais grape.

LES COMPAGNONS DU BEAUJOLAIS

The first of these brotherhoods, and the mother of all of them, is the Confréries des Compagnons du Beaujolais, created soon after the last war, in 1949.

The Fellows, *Compagnons*, are administered by a committee, headed at present by M de Rambuteau. They are in no sense an organization dedicated to folklore, although the members of the committee appear at the various enthronement ceremonies dressed in traditional costumes; that is, round felt hats, green canvas aprons, and black jackets. At their

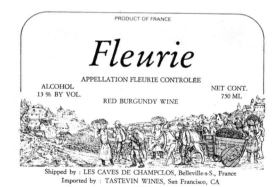

PAVILLON DE L'ÉLYSÉE

EX - LANGER

Jardins des Champs-Elysées

ANJOU 29-60 & 85-10
P A R I S   VIII ᵉ

four gatherings, *Tenues* (one per season), they oblige candidates for the brotherhood to drink from giant goblets, *tastevins*, whose content is symbolic; after which they are dubbed on the shoulder with a vine branch, and a silver *tasse* (wine-tasting cup) is hung round their necks by a green cord. Then the candidate is presented with his diploma and signs a register.

But the goals pursued by the *Compagnons* go far beyond their motto – *Vuydons les Tonnaux* (let us drain the barrels). The oath sworn by each new *compagnon* before he goes up to the altar, under the impassive gaze of a wooden Saint-Vincent, is this:

'I swear before Saint-Vincent to behave as a faithful and free *Compagnon de Beaujolais* and to practise the virtues of such. My duty is to love our country, to work to uphold its traditions of hospitality, wisdom and good humour. To make known the beauty of its beautiful places, and the interest of its old churches and ancient *châteaux*, which bear witness to a past enriched by the spirit of its artists and builders. To appreciate and to disseminate the produce of our vines. Lastly, to honour the rugged wine-growers who, by their good work, have forged the prosperity and the reward of our Beaujolais homeland. . . .'

At each enthronement, and in the presence of their 500 guests, the *compagnons* invariably link their association with the great historical tradition of *Compagnonnage*; namely, *savour-faire*, solidarity and fraternity. The wine of the Beaujolais, whose eleven *appellations* take turns presiding over enthronements and reunions, does the rest – which is to say, it spreads a spirit of optimism,

166

generosity and satisfaction. Thus the revelation experienced by Edouard Herriot one evening at his office on the Quai d'Orsay becomes fact:

'Men have long searched for the original site of Earthly paradise. Scholars, seek no more. Beyond all shadow of doubt, the Garden of Adam and Eve lay close to Quincié, between the valley and the hillcrest. And it was no apple that tempted the first woman. It was a grape. How willingly I pardon her, and how well I understand.'

The *Compagnons du Beaujolais* are to some extent the prophets of that paradise. Since one cannot carry away one's homeland, far less a paradise, on the soles of one's shoes, some of the *Compagnons* have created subsidiaries, known in their language as *devoirs*. Thus there is a *devoir* in Paris. Its members perpetuate the glorious days of the first free French combatants in London. Jean Oberle liked to relate how, during the terrible winter of 1940–41, the first Frenchmen who joined Général de Gaulle sometimes sank into the deepest melancholy. They would try to raise one another's spirits with remarks like: 'The Beaujolais was really admirable at La Mascotte, on Rue des Abbesses' . . . 'I beg your pardon, it was better Chez Ducottier, in the Halle aux Vins'. There is also a Mediterranean *devoir*, one of whose

centres is the Hôtel de la Tour, at Sanary; a Swiss *devoir*, which makes nonsense of the pejorative French expression 'to drink like a Swiss', and others more or less throughout the world: in Germany, England, Belgium, the USA and Canada. Their members are citizens of two nations; one is that of their ancestors – and the other, which they have imbibed, is the Beaujolais.

THE PRAYER OF THE COMPAGNONS

One evening in January 1949, at the Château de Pizay, the *Compagnons du Beaujolais* assembled (both believers and disbelievers) to hear Jean Guillermet read the prayer written for them by the Abbé Pradel. This prayer was inspired by a blend of early Christian visions, the Bible, and the Song of Songs; delivered in the wild accents of Péguy and with true Bacchic ardour, it offers a clear definition of what the *Confrérie des Compagnons* is all about. Their primary concern is to defend and promote the area, *Terroir*, its landscapes, its vineyards, and its people. In this there is an almost religious implication.

'It is very meet, right, and our bounden duty, that we should at all times and places give thanks unto thee Holy Lord, Father Almighty, Eternal God . . .

167

'But on this day of great and joyous festivity, we give thee thanks that, according to thy will, the sun hath formed upon the hillsides through which the children of men may hold captive unto themselves all the overflowings of its glory . . .

'To the Holy Tree of the vine hast thou given power and lordship over the rays of the daystar, to receive them and blend them with her sap, that we may gather with our hands and drink with our lips the precious and fleeting warmth of the sun . . .

'We give thanks to Thee, O Lord, for all the warmth enclosed in the cool of our cellars.

'We give thanks to Thee, O Lord, for that thy prophets have written that thou wast beloved of a wife, and that thy wife was a vine (. . .)

'We give thanks to Thee, O Lord, for the golden vine which rose up before the gates of thy holy Temple in Jerusalem, in the guise of thy holy nation, as a wife in supplication before her husband . . .

'For by thy union, O Lord, all the vines of the world have been blessed.

'We give thee thanks, O Lord, that to announce the great change desired by all men, thy son did turn six vessels of water into generous wine . . . and that He did choose this fruit of the vine to pour into our innermost being the Blood of his triumphant and living Cross.

'O Lord, we give thee thanks for all the grapes that die for the greater joy and strength of mankind, and for the joy of those who drink . . .

'And for the Mystery of thy Christ, who died for the lives of many and who spoke of the new wine that His disciples would drink in the Kingdom of Heaven . . . and who spoke of new wine each time He announced the coming of the Kingdom of Heaven . . . and again spoke of it on the last night . . .

'And we ask thy blessing, O Lord, on the sun-drenched earth all covered in green vines, which also is blessed by Our Lady in her Chapel of Brouilly, the mother of a Messiah who said these words to His friends gathered for the last supper:

'I am the true vine, and my father is the husbandman. . . .'

MOUNT SINAI IN THE BEAUJOLAIS

One Saturday, around four in the afternoon, some walkers who had climbed the slopes of a mountain covered in vines, were surprised to discover about sixty fellows seated around a table at the top. They wielded their forks with gusto and washed down cold sausages and ham with long draughts of red wine, which must have been delicious, if their prodigious consumption was anything to go by.

This happened at Brouilly, one of the greatest feathers in the cap of the Beaujolais. If you climb this mountain, you will witness a panorama which is among the loveliest in France, a country by no means ill-endowed with views.

The sixty men had climbed Mont Brouilly for a solemn ceremony in honour of the wine of the Beaujolais. I had been summoned by invitation, and as a good citizen of Lyon, familiar since my youth with fine wines, I was able to give a reasonable account of myself in this assembled company.

When we had reached the cheese, a speech was made which ended thus:

'The people from the Ain — we're sorry they're not here. But we are cordially grateful to our Mâconnais guests for coming: and we consider their presence a compliment to our hills. As for all these men of the Beaujolais I see around me, what can I say? They all know us inside out, since there isn't one, I think, with whom I haven't emptied many a bottle. And if there is, let him stand up, and I will instantly give him satisfaction, though I may lie snoring on the field as a result.'

This personation was greeted with roars of approval by the company, who knew the mystique that had inspired it . . . united by countless local bonds, they made up a fine assortment of Beaujolais types. But clouds were threatening to

cast a premature pall over the day, and it seemed already as if the light was wavering, as indeed was the landscape before the eyes of my fellow-pilgrims. At this moment a voice, seeming to come from the mists, was heard by the faithful as they waited on their Sinai:

'Go forth and speak in my name. Go forth and graft. Go forth and drink toasts. Go forth, and by the virtues of my wine, fortify those who are weak, warm those who are cold, cheer those who are sad, console those who are in misery, and bring love, concord and joy wherever you go. Go forth and recruit. And each year I shall come back among you and find you more numerous.'

Was the voice human or divine? I shall never know, because most of us were lost in a vague joy of fervent ecstasy. But one real miracle did occur: not one of the worshippers who had climbed that hill a few hours earlier came down it on the seat of his trousers. A proof that Bacchus takes care of the people of the Beaujolais. A proof that he keeps a helping hand on their coat tails, when the road is not straight, and has given them good wives with good sense, who know how to say merely: t'as encore bu un coup, mon homme? *(had another drink, my man?) – without making it an affair of state or grounds for divorce.*

It must be said that the people of this place don't have bad wine, because Beaujolais is a damn good wine which never did anyone any harm. The more you drink of it, the kinder seems your wife, the more faithful your friends, the rosier your future and the more bearable humanity. All the evil in the world is because of one fact: there is only one Beaujolais on the face of the planet. It is here that the elect may be found (and they are few in number, as we know).

GABRIEL CHEVALLIER
EXTRAIT DE *BROUILLY*, DE JUSTIN DUTRAIVE, 1979

'GOSIERS SECS' *AND* 'GRAPILLEURS'

The Beaujolais owes much to two other *Confréries*: the *Gosiers Secs de Clochemerle* (the dry-gullets of Clochemerle) and the *Grapilleurs des Pierres Dorées* (gleaners of the Pierres Dorées).

These two associations both seek to set up a *terroir* within a *terroir*. Though united as a body, the Beaujolais is actually made up of a series of tiny areas of climates, *Climats*, and the many *appellations* are justified in many nuances of taste. But this diversity is also perceptible in the countryside and in the people's outlook.

The southern Beaujolais, within a triangle which broadly covers the area between Villefranche, Lamure and L'Arbresle, has a strong originality of its own. This derives, first of all, from the stone, which is the colour of good fresh bread; all the villages are built of it, and the chequerboard of vineyards, divided by drystone walls, has its tint. The gentle inclines of the valleys give this country of ochre sandstone a special beauty. Here are woodlands as well as vines, which add an element of silence and intimacy. There are also plenty of *Garrigues*, areas of rough vegetation, which are used for raising goats for the production of a cheese which goes well with the local wine. Mushrooms gathered in the woods add a distinctive flavour to the local dishes of *civet au capucin* (jugged hare) or *coq au vin*.

The yellow houses with their Roman tiles, the churches, the *châteaux*, the wayside crosses and the *cadoles*, those doll's houses one sees at the corners of the vineyards, all combine to produce a landscape reflecting the patience and hard work of the men who live in it. Even its legends of haunted dungeons, dark forests and gloomy crypts have the air of fireside confidences. Most of all perhaps, the originality of the *Pays des Pierres Dorées* lies in its balance of custom, scenery and history. It is a kind of Beaujolais *Touraine*, a place that knows how to live well.

The latter science – innate of course – is what the *Grapilleurs des*

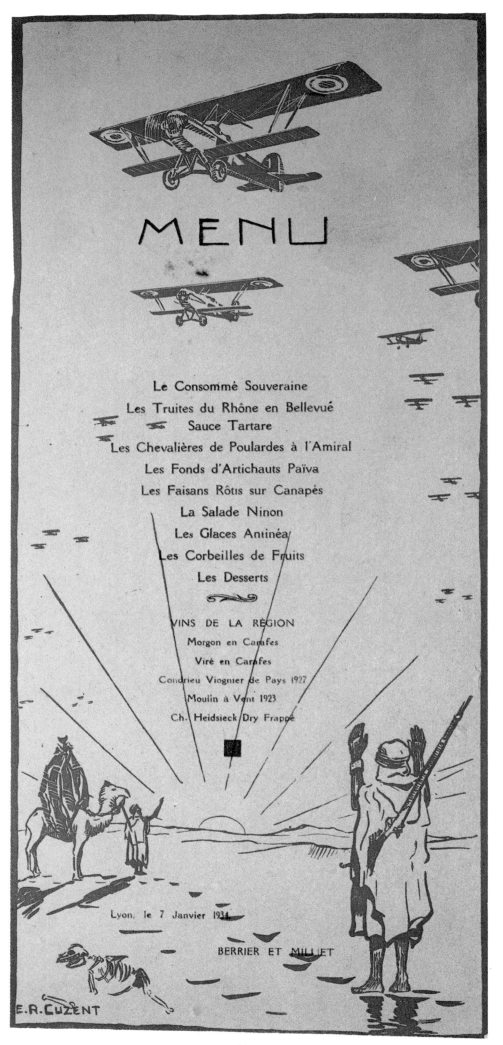

MENU

Le Consommé Souveraine

Les Truites du Rhône en Bellevué
Sauce Tartare

Les Chevalières de Poulardes à l'Amiral

Les Fonds d'Artichauts Païva

Les Faisans Rôtis sur Canapés

La Salade Ninon

Les Glaces Antinéa

Les Corbeilles de Fruits

Les Desserts

VINS DE LA RÉGION

Morgon en Carafes

Viré en Carafes

Condrieu Viognier de Pays 1927

Moulin à Vent 1923

Ch. Heidsieck Dry Frappé

Lyon, le 7 Janvier 1934

BERRIER ET MILLIET

E.R. CUZENT

20ᵉ
Anniversaire de la «Grappe Fleurie»

La Grappe Fleurie

Menu

La Terrine du Chef

Le Gratin de Fruits de Mer

Le Rôti de Porc aux Pruneaux

Les Fromages

La Tarte aux Pommes

Vin de Fleurie

MAISON DES BEAUJOLAIS
Le Samedi 2 Janvier 1971

Attends, mon Vieux !

....   Un doigt, deux doigts et je me grise
Quand j'y descends, je marche droit.   A moi le mur, le pilier ?
De mon vieux vin, je bois un doigt,   Je ne trouve plus l'escalier.

"All right, all right, you've convinced us — we'll take the Beaujolais!"

172

BROUILLY
Appellation contrôlée

DOMAINE DE CONROY
Mᵐᵉ de Saint-Charles, propriétaire à Odenas (Rhône) 75 cl

SÉLECTIONNÉ ET MIS EN BOUTEILLE AU DOMAINE PAR
LES VINS GEORGES DUBŒUF, ROMANÈCHE-THORINS - 71

RÉCOLTE
1984
Beaujolais Nouveau

APPELLATION BEAUJOLAIS CONTRÔLÉE

ALC. 12.5 % VOL.   70 cl

Sélectionné et mis en bouteille par LES VINS MATHELIN à 69 Châtillon-d'Azergues France
PRODUIT DE FRANCE

Pierres Dorées try to communicate when they entertain visitors who have fallen in love with their district and its wines. The *Gosiers Secs*, by contrast, are based at Haux-en-Beaujolais, acknowledged to be the original of Gabriel Chevallier's famous *Clochemerle*. Here the enthronements tend to be more robust, the initiate needs a strong constitution, a taste for risks, and a profound knowledge of the *Clochemerle* saga, born between a public urinal and a completely phony cure, in which the real Curé Ponosse is none other than the king of the Beaujolais chitterling, a certain Bobosse. But here, as elsewhere, the local wine is synonymous with revelry and good fellowship. Even the administration makes its contribution. I remember that during a recent meeting of the *Gosiers Secs*, the people who ran the Haut-Clochemerle Café had suffered a bereavement. There was no question of the tavern opening that day. But what would become of our party, if there was no place to go for a drink after the meeting? No problem: the Mayor ceded us the town hall for the evening, and there we continued to talk of Beaujolais after we had drunk it . . . The *Amis de Brouilly* are another typical Beaujolais association in the same world, though not exactly a brotherhood. Each year at the end of the summer when the harvest is about to begin, the Friends of Brouilly invite all lovers of Beaujolais to climb Mont Brouilly. When they reach the top of this local Ararat, they gather around the chapel of Notre-Dame du Raisin which has guarded the health of the grapes for over 130 years. Their rallying cry is a song:

> *Si le temps est beau,*
> *Il faut monter là-haut,*
> *Tu verras Montmerle . . .*

The only obligation to participants is that they must bring along their own food. Bread, wine and salt are served in unlimited quantities on tables round which people sit wherever they like, enjoying the glorious view of the Beaujolais and the Saône valley. As the hours go by, new friendships are made and the air is filled with good talk and good fellowship. Everyone here has already accepted the rule:

BROUILLY
PISSE VIEILLE
APPELLATION BROUILLY CONTROLÉE

Produit de France

Jean LATHUILIÈRE 75 cl
Viticulteur à CERCIÉ (Rhône)

MISE EN BOUTEILLES A LA PROPRIÉTÉ

MOULIN-A-VENT
APPELLATION MOULIN-A-VENT CONTRÔLÉE

COMTE DE SPARRE, PROPRIÉTAIRE A CHÉNAS (RHONE) FRANCE

SÉLECTIONNÉ ET MIS EN BOUTEILLES AU DOMAINE PAR
LES VINS GEORGES DUBŒUF A 71720 ROMANÈCHE-THORINS 75 cl

Savour Club

Saint-Amour
1982
APPELLATION SAINT-AMOUR CONTRÔLÉE

MIS EN BOUTEILLE A ROMANÈCHE-THORINS
PAR LE SAVOUR CLUB, NÉGOCIANT A LANCIÉ (RHÔNE)

PRODUCE
OF FRANCE
Savour Club   75 cl

PRODUCT OF FRANCE

Château Lagrange Cochard
MORGON
APPELLATION MORGON CONTRÔLÉE   75 cl
Mis en bouteille par
LES CAVES DE CHAMPCLOS
Belleville-sur-Saône (Rh.) France

Cuvée des Amis du

CLUB MERCEDES BENZ DE FRANCE

BEAUJOLAIS
APPELLATION CONTROLEE

75 cl   Produce of France

mis en bouteilles par

Antoine Depagneux à Villefranche (Rhône)

174

LE BEAUJOL

J'aime beaucoup le mois de mai
Le mois d'aimer dans le muguet
Mais la saison que je préfère
C'est la saison des cimetières
Non pas pour déposer des fleurs
Sur ceux qui dorment dans mon cœur
Mais pour donner un coup d'palais
Dans le beaujolais.

C'est l'instant où Bacchus enfin
Nous donne son enfant divin
C'est l'heure où dans la chapelle
Autour des foudres de l'autel
La bande de cons bons enfants
Va taster religieusement
Le nouveau-né qu'on attendait
Notre beaujolais.

Malheur à l'intrus qui surgit
Au cours de la cérémonie
Au diable tous les faux goûteurs
Les m'as-tu-vu de connaisseurs
Ce n'est pas un cocktail mondain
Ni du folklore pour pantins
Mais une orgie de fins goulets
Au p'tit beaujolais.

C'est notre credo notre foi
Beaujol beaujol je crois en toi
C'est notre cri de ralliement
A beaujol on répond présent
C'est notre Pâque, notre Cène
C'est notre exorciseur de peine
Le magicien de nos pamphlets
Ce cher beaujolais.

O miracle et enchantement
La foi produit des faits troublants
Voilà que nous descend du ciel
Bacchus notre père éternel
Euterpe pendue à son bras
Fin saoule nous donne le La
Et c'est parti pour un couplet
Sacré beaujolais.

Si le monde tourne à l'envers
Depuis des décennies ma mère
C'est parce qu'à cette saison
Tout le paradis est fin rond
Il paraît que le vin d'ici
Éloigne l'eau de là et si
Vous prisez cet air guilleret
A moi vous ne devez rien mais
Tout au beaujolais.

Song written and put to music by Robert Grange

C'est là que, posément, ils s'empliront la panse,
Que toujours soit honni celui qui mal y pense . . .

Later, as evening draws on, the wiser guests withdraw to the valley, but there always remains a die-hard lust of revellers, who decide to keep the evening going.

At dawn the next day, they will be seen emerging from some local cellar, still exchanging vows of eternal friendship. . . .

COME TO THE BEAUJOLAIS

The activities of the brotherhoods are supported and complemented by folk groups who perform only drinking songs, but also songs in praise of the countryside of the Beaujolais. Among these groups are: the *Cadets du Beaujolais* at Villefranche; the *Grappe Fleurie* at Fleurie; and the *Chansonnière du Beaujolais*, run by the composer Claude Morel at Châtillon-d'Azergues.

Other celebrants of the region are its poets, who have always been assiduous in its praises, and particularly in praise of its wine. Such as Emile de Villié:

Mon ami! Qui ne boit qu'un seul verre est boiteux:
Il n'a rien qu'une jambe! Il en faut au moins deux!
'Bis repetita placent' dit un juste adage!
Le premier verre est bon, l'autre l'est davantage!
Comme un magicien le noble vin s'avère.
Car fusses-tu plus laid qu'un singe ou qu'un corbeau,
Si tu pouvais te voir au travers de ton verre,
Tu te trouverais beau!

We would also cite the works of Francisque Norgelet, Pierre Aguétant and Léon Foillard, always remembering that Victor Hugo himself was moved to passion by the women gathering grapes in the Beaujolais. '. . . *ces cultivatrices penchées sur les vignes et dont on voyait surtout la première syllabe.*'

Come to the Beaujolais; you will find the descendants of Toine Dumontot awaiting you at their cellar doors, with the words:

SAINT-AMOUR
APPELLATION CONTROLÉE

RÉCOLTE 1980

CE VIN A OBTENU LE PRIX BACCHUS, RÉCOMPENSE ACCORDÉE AU MEILLEUR BEAUJOLAIS LORS DU CONCOURS DES VINS DE LA SAINT-VINCENT A MACON, LE 24 JANVIER 1981

SÉLECTIONNÉ ET MIS EN BOUTEILLES PAR
GEORGES DUBŒUF   75 cl
ROMANÈCHE-THORINS, SAONE-ET-LOIRE, FRANCE

177

Національный консоммé
Ліонскія пулярды
Семьга изъ Люары съ кисейнымъ соусомъ
Козуля по Суворовски
Нантуйскія тимбали
——о——
Кликотовскіе граниты
——о——
Фазаны съ овсянкой
Горошокъ по-французски
Пирогъ изъ гусиной печени съ труфлями
Московскій саладъ
Кронштадтское мороженое
Дессеръ

ВИНА

Моргонъ въ графинахъ—Мадера съ острова
Шато Ситранъ 1878 — Мутонъ Ротшильдъ
Помаръ 1885 — Шамбертенъ 1885
Дюкъ Монтебелло Гранъ Креманъ

Ліонъ. Типографія А. Шторка

Juliénas
Appellation Contrôlée
AUJOUX & Cⁱᵉ A Sᵗ GEORGES DE RENEINS (RH)

PRODUIT DE FRANCE

Domaine du Petit Pérou
MORGON
APPELLATION MORGON CONTROLÉE   75 cl

Mis en bouteille par
LES CAVES DE CHAMPCLOS, Belleville-sur-Saône - Rhône

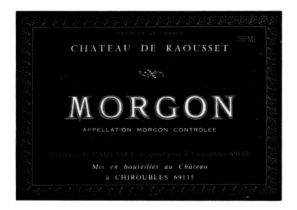

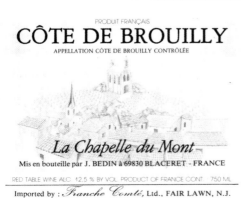

cover. Bring to the boil, then pour into a large casserole, cover and cook till done.

Chamour derives from a word in the local dialect meaning a sort of solid pumpkin flan. This was formerly a dish offered to the grape harvesters in generous measure, so generous that these seasonal workers came to be known as *Chamouris*. *Chamour* was made in the Biblical fashion: boil pieces of a large pumpkin till fairly soft; when done, remove from the water and dry carefully. Then mash with a fork, mixing in two or three piled tablespoonfuls of crushed biscuits. Sugar and salt lightly, and add a generous handful of white flour and two or three beaten eggs. Mix well and place in a large earthenware pan which can go in the oven without cracking. Scatter breadcrumbs over the top, with plenty of butter, then cook in a medium oven until a knife can be pushed into the *Chamour* and come out clean.

Pognou is a delicacy made with bread dough, mixed up with plenty of butter and a little sugar, to which are added (according to the season) cherries and slices of apple or pear. This, when baked, produces a heavy cake, excellent served with a very cool Beaujolais.

Saucisson au Vin was not made with ordinary sausage, but with the country version, cut thick and cooked in a stewpot in pure Beaujolais. To this was added coarse ground pepper, a bunch of thyme and some cinnamon.

This simple cuisine is what people ate at home. It never reached the restaurants, and it dates from the time of those memorable end-of-harvest or end-of-pressing banquets. The wine-growers' wives used to excel themselves at these glorious feasts: *Saucisson au vin, Boeuf bouilli, Chapon au bouillon gras* (Capon) served with a huge platter of rice . . . and *Chamour* as a side-dish, vegetable or dessert. As a digestive, a liqueur wine known as *L'Ami de l'Homme* would be served; this was a kind of Beaujolais elixir, composed of sweet white wine from the press to which one glassful per litre of old *marc* was added (not to be confused with the deadly *rikiki*).

Well may we thank our Lady of Brouilly for all these good things. Thanks to her intervention, miracles can still happen.

Recent initiatives have shown that nothing can restrain gastronomic research from continuing its progress. For example, only recently, M Gérard Chaut, of Chamelet, is said to have invented a new kind of *grappille*, based on a mixture of nuts, honey and marc.

LES COCHONNAILLES DU PAYS

Any *saucisson* worthy of the name is conscientiously and affectionately made. They are eaten at christenings, weddings and funerals . . . and many people consume them in the early morning for breakfast. In the Beaujolais, much fuss is made over the *rosette* of sausage, which is taken with the wine of the same year. The *rosette* is a high quality sausage, proud of being embossed in the rectum of the pig – hence its name, because a pig's anus has a certain resemblance to a rose, and even to a certain French official decoration.

The Jemo sausage, to take an example, arrives swaddled in a kind of net; the meat is contained in a part of the pig's intestine, and while drying takes the plump shape of a doll – hence its name.

Among the hot sausages, nothing could be better than *Andouillettes Tirées à la Ficelle*, as they are prepared in the marvellous charcuteries along the Calade. These *andouillettes* have made the reputation of the exquisite René Besson, known as 'Bobosse', an important regional figure who has lately acquired an international standing from his base at Saint-Jean-D'Ardières. His *andouillettes* are based on the calf's crow, and never cause any trouble to people with delicate stomachs. A course of grilled *andouillettes* is even cited as a cure for dyspepsia.

All that remains to describe is the oily *Sabodet*, with its distant Dauphinois origins. This is a pot-bellied sausage, stuffed with pork rind and jowls. It is eaten well cooked, still wet from the hot bouillon, and it is

BALLADE DES FROMAGES DE CHÈVRES

Doux comme un miel de l'Hélicon,
Les fromages de la fermière,
Vont, bien rangés dans leur panière,
Au marché de Villié-Morgon.
Las ! Ils ont quitté leur chaumière
Aussi restent-ils tout pâlots
D'avoir laissé les sapinières
De Marchampt ou des Écharmeaux.

Ce sont les petits chevrotons
Plus fins que le plus fin gruyère,
Ressource de la cuisinière
Après le gigot de mouton.
Parfois durs comme de la pierre
Ou tendres comme du gâteau,
On croit respirer la bruyère
De Marchampt ou des Écharmeaux.

Fernand Velon: extract from Le pays et le Vin
Beaujolais *by Léon Foillard and Tony David,*
1929

served on a bed of lentils. All these *cochonnailles* have inspired the poets of the Beaujolais and given good reasons for returning there to many a trencherman. The brilliant Colette, remembering an evening spent at Brouilly with Claude Geoffray, the lord of Château-Thivin, wrote: '. . . our meal was a homage to hams well wrapped in fat, sausages like new leather, and a certain cheese, referred to as *fort*, which provokes an unslakeable thirst.'

THE CANARD ENCHAÎNÉ *AT JULIÉNAS*

The fame of Juliénas in the columns of the mischievous *Canard Enchaîné* dates from the 1930s. It is still heavily featured and this admirable publication acts as a Beaujolais bridgehead to Paris. The link derives from an enthusiastic friendship between Toto Dubois and Victor Peyret, both of whom are now dead. Before devoting himself to the vines of Juliénas, Toto Dubois was a journalist at the Lyon Salut Public. He had fought in the First World War, during which he had come to know Maurice Maréchal, the future head of the *Canard Enchaîné*. (The *Canard* started out as a simple gazette distributed in the trenches.) Maréchal, hearing that his friend was living at Juliénas, came to see him, and subsequently brought along his most talented journalists: those who liked good wine. Toto Dubois offered so generous a welcome that the *Canard*'s pilgrimage became a regular occurrence. Henri Quilas designed the menu for the Coq au Vin restaurant, and during one famous lunch there on September 29, 1934, the entire editorial staff of the *Canard* was present: Maréchal, Tréno, Pol Ferjac, Pierre Bénard, Pruvost, Pédro, Quilac, Pavil and many more.

Victor Peyret was Toto Dubois' successor; he was a grower at the Château des Capitans at Juliénas. Peyret was also a great lover of arts and letters, and the founder of the Cellier de la Vieille Eglise. He never missed a chance to join the feasts arranged for the *Canard*, nor to visit their offices when he passed through

Paris. His contribution to Juliénas has been recognized in our own time by the 1965 attribution of a Victor Peyret Prize, which is given every year in mid-November, at the Fête des Vins. Naturally, associates of the *Canard Enchaîné* have often been among the prizewinners.

The back of the famous *1934* menu at the Coq au Vin, inscribed by the journalists of *the* Canard Enchaîné

ACKNOWLEDGEMENTS

The authors and publishers would like to thank the following for supplying material:

Mme DARGENT,

Mme DEVELAY,

P. AUDRAS,

H. BESSON,

BRAULT,

G. CANARD,

G. CLAUDEY,

G. COMPARAT,

J.-L. DESVIGNES,

G. DUBŒUF,

P. FAURE,

J. FEU,

PH. FOURNEAU,

A. GOUGENHEIM,

CH. MÉRIEUX,

P. MARINGUE,

ORSI,

M. PASQUIER-DESVIGNES

P. PERICHON-MESLAY,

F. ROSTAING,

P. SARRAU,

J. TIXIER,

J.-P. THORIN,

L'Union interprofessionnelle des vins du Beaujolais,

Le Centre d'Arts et Traditions Populaires de Villefranche-sur-Saône